WOMEN

& RETIREMENT PLANNING

WOMEN
& RETIREMENT PLANNING

Understanding Retirement Plans, Investment Choices, and Retirement Plan Distributions

Donald S. Gudhus, MBA Carol J. Ventura, MBA, CFP®

iUniverse LLC
Bloomington

WOMEN & RETIREMENT PLANNING
UNDERSTANDING RETIREMENT PLANS, INVESTMENT CHOICES, AND RETIREMENT PLAN DISTRIBUTIONS

iUniverse books may be ordered through booksellers or by contacting:

iUniverse
1663 Liberty Drive
Bloomington, IN 47403
www.iuniverse.com
1-800-Authors (1-800-288-4677)

Because of the dynamic nature of the Internet, any web addresses or links contained in this book may have changed since publication and may no longer be valid. The views expressed in this work are solely those of the author and do not necessarily reflect the views of the publisher, and the publisher hereby disclaims any responsibility for them.

Any people depicted in stock imagery provided by Thinkstock are models, and such images are being used for illustrative purposes only.

Certain stock imagery © Thinkstock

ISBN: 978-1-4759-8805-5 (sc)
ISBN: 978-1-4759-8806-2 (e)

Library of Congress Control Number: 2013907782

Printed in the United States of America.

iUniverse rev. date: 7/19/13

Dedicated to our families.

ENDORSEMENTS

A "must read" for anyone with an IRA or other retirement account, this book is chock-full of practical solutions for retirement savings, and the authors have effectively translated highly complex rules and regulations that apply to retirement accounts into "Plain English."

—Denise Appleby, CISP, CRC, CRPS, CRSP, APA; IRA
expert, consultant, and author, Grayson, GA

Women & Retirement Planning is an excellent do-it-yourself guide for those who may be entering the vast world of retirement finance. The book's direction to women is perfect in an era when women have not only claimed their places in all areas of the business world but in independently directing their own financial lives.

Having worked in the finance business for many years as both stockbroker and independent financial advisor, I still found this book to be a helpful guide to the various approaches to retirement and to the investments available and appropriate for each plan. It presents retirement issues and the pros and cons of the various plans in a down-to-earth, easy-to-read manner that makes a seemingly complicated subject a "walk in the park."

I could also envision this book as a valuable resource for advisors to present to their clients—male or female—for reading prior to their discussions regarding the setup of their plans. It is one thing, particularly for a client who is visiting this issue for the first time, to listen to an advisor's recommendations for retirement planning; it is another to have read a complete comparison of the options, as this book presents them, and to begin with a clear picture in your own head of the choices within your own comfort level. I compliment Don and Carol on their thorough analyses and explanations of the options for retirement plans and investments, and I think its reach can be useful to women and beyond.

—M. Lois Brown, financial consultant and founder, Investcheck, Philadelphia, PA

Confused about how to choose which mutual funds are the best choice for your retirement savings? Wondering whether you should save in a Roth IRA, traditional IRA, or 401(k)? *Women & Retirement Planning* is a straightforward, easy-to-understand, yet comprehensive guide to investing for retirement. Whether you're just starting to save, are a mid-career worker, or are on the verge of retirement, this book offers useful, in-depth answers to questions you're likely to have. And it does it without skimping on the technical details that are essential knowledge for savvy investors. Plus, tables throughout the book make it easy to compare the pros and cons of, for example, the various types of IRAs, and to weigh the differences between traditional mutual funds versus exchange-traded funds. Retirement is no longer about simply moving from work to leisure. Nowadays, retirement might last two decades or more and funding it is, usually, up to you. In *Women & Retirement Planning,* Don Gudhus and Carol Ventura provide an essential guidebook for savers facing the brave new world of retirement.

—Andrea Coombes, personal finance writer/editor, San Francisco,
CA; winner of the 2012 Excellence in Personal Finance Reporting
Award from the Radio Television Digital News Association;
writer, MarketWatch and other business-news publications

Donald Gudhus and Carol Ventura have recognized the special needs of women for advice and deep knowledge about long-term investment planning and how to structure their finances for retirement. They write clearly about what sometimes seems hopelessly complicated. This book goes a long way toward making the very complex world of long-term investing and retirement planning understandable for a very broad range of people.

—Stephen J. Friedman, president, Pace University, New York, NY

Ladies, our future financial survival depends on our ability to accept responsibility for our needs. Don Gudhus and Carol Ventura pack a lot of practical information into a small space. All women should keep this book in a place that they can lay their hands on it every time a retirement decision is necessary.

—Joy Kirsch, CFP® and founder of the non-profit
The Widow's Journey, Bedford, TX

This book will enable you to better understand and to pursue your retirement and financial goals by becoming a savvier investor. Anyone who saves for retirement must read this book.

—Gary S. Lesser, author, *Roth IRA Answer Book*, Indianapolis, IN

The authors' expertise and practical advice provide valuable insight into a critical topic. This book should be required reading for every woman.

—Sally Mulhern, Esq., author, *Estate Planning to Die For®: An Insider's Guide for Financial Professionals*, Portsmouth, NH

This book is very comprehensive, especially the retirement plan descriptions. It is an excellent treatise or reference guide for advisors and investors. Its simple descriptions are excellent.

—Roger Ochs, president, H.D. Vest Inc., Irving, TX

ACKNOWLEDGMENTS

From Don Gudhus:
My brother Dennis and other family members provided the kind inspiration and support requisite to undertaking the writing of another book. Also, my clients at Oracle Financial Group provided the kind of encouragement that can't be found anywhere else. It's through them that many analyses and tested ideas have been successfully implemented. To all, many, many thanks.

From Carol Ventura:
Thank you to Bill Henry, Herb Vest, Barbara Hancock, and Roger Ochs for encouraging pursuit of advanced designations and degrees as well as providing an environment to learn and strengthen my skills. My appreciation to Susan Hartnett, Carol Gransee, Judy Tarpley, and Kathryn Capage for being my mentors. To the staff at PenServ Inc. and Gary Lesser for answering all of my very detailed questions throughout the years.

CONTENTS

INTRODUCTION

It's not what you earn, it's what you keep.

Warren Buffett,
CEO and chairman,
Berkshire Hathaway

In Prudential's[1] tenth-anniversary publication, "Financial Experience & Behaviors among Women," the researchers state that women are becoming increasingly aware, engaged, and actively involved in their finances. The study shows an upward trend in the role of women as the key decision maker in their household—an incredible 95 percent are financial decision makers. Eighty four percent of married women are either solely or jointly responsible for household financial decisions. So where are the books and publications to help those women, who have been historically underserved, make the final decisions that will determine long-term financial security for themselves and their families?

Well, you could read Don's 2008 book, *Women & Mutual Funds: Gain Understanding and Be in Control,* in which you can learn about mutual funds and the development of a portfolio. Or, before learning about mutual funds and portfolio building, which the authors recommend, read *Women & Retirement Planning: Understanding Retirement Plans, Investment Choices, and Retirement Plan Distributions,* and have at your fingertips an immense amount of usable information about retirement plans and related issues and the answers to a vast array of questions about your retirement plans,

---

1   "Financial Experience & Behaviors among Women: 2010–2011." Prudential Research Study. Newark, NJ: The Prudential Insurance Company of America. 10th Anniversary Edition, 2010.

including: Why should I invest in a Roth IRA? Am I investing in the best retirement plans for me? Have I selected the best mutual funds for my 401(k)? When can I start taking distributions from my retirement plans? What is the best way to take these distributions? What are the income tax implications of taking distributions? These answers and more are contained within the following pages. Read on.

Planning for retirement fifty years ago was simple—when your first job was your one and only job. The above questions didn't have to be asked. If you were in a nonunion position, retirement was taken care of by the company's defined benefit plan and the government's Social Security benefit. If your work was overseen by a union, retirement income consisted of the union's pension and Social Security. If you needed any additional income, you made the effort to save during your working years.

Nowadays, things are a bit more complex. Defined benefit plans, while still in existence, are a virtual relic. Very few companies have them. Social Security remains viable, but for how long? The burden for your retirement has become your burden. No longer is planning for retirement the so-called responsibility of your company and the government.

To help you out, however, the government introduced additional ways to save for retirement. There is the IRA, which can either be a Roth or a traditional IRA; 401(k); 403(b); 457; SEP-IRA; profit sharing, money purchase; cash balance; defined benefit; SIMPLE; SARSEP; Thrift; and so on. As the late Phil Rizzuto, former New York Yankee shortstop, member of the Baseball Hall of Fame, and announcer, would exclaim, "Holy Cow!"

What is all this? How do you know what's good, what's best for you?

Well, you've come to the right place.

What Retirement Plan Is Best for You?

Unfortunately, it's not possible for us to say what's best for you. Why? Because we don't know you personally—what you do, your personal and family needs, desires, goals, earning power, tolerance for risk, time frame to achieve your goals, and so on.

What we have done, however, is offer a detailed description of each of the plans that are available. If you're an individual employee, you'll be able to determine the best plan for yourself. Could it be a Roth IRA combined with your company's 401(k)? Or is it a traditional IRA combined with your organization's 403(b)? If you're a small business owner/entrepreneur, you'll see the plans that may be best for you. Maybe it's a Roth IRA and a defined benefit plan. Perhaps it's a traditional IRA combined with a money purchase plan. If you're an executive, you'll find the plans that are best for you. Could it possibly be a traditional IRA, a 457, a 401(k), and a defined benefit plan?

Choosing the best plan or plans is extremely important. Normally, one does not make this decision too many times. Typically, such a decision is made only when there is a significant lifestyle change. So be careful and choose wisely.

Why Should You Participate?

The cost of retirement will probably continue to escalate every year. Health-care costs will experience significant increases. Food costs will rise. Housing costs probably will not go lower. Entertainment costs will go up. And so on …

Furthermore, people are living longer. In the *Journal of Financial Service Professionals*, Ronald F. Duska, PhD, states, "Fifty years ago, when average life expectancy was 65, retirement was not much of an anxiety-producing event. In those days, if one lived past that age, retirement seemed like an extended vacation. However, with average life expectancy currently hovering at 85, a retirement when one's age is in the late 60s or early 70s leaves the possibility of a person living another quarter of a century."[2] For example, in 1970, a forty-year-old female could expect to live 37.8 more years. Today, a forty-year-old female in the United States can expect to live another 40.8 years to 80.8 years.[3] So not only are yearly retirement costs rising, retirement costs are increasing because women are living longer also.

How can this dilemma of managing the cost of retirement be addressed? One way is by participating in the plans that are best for you, choosing your investments wisely, and investing regularly. (While investing regularly will help you accumulate retirement assets over time, this form of investing may not protect your account from losses in a declining market or guarantee a profit. As such, it's important to be mindful of your ability to sustain a regular and frequent investment plan even in periods of declining markets.)

---

2   Duska, Ronald F., PhD. "On Helping Your Retirees." *Journal of Financial Service Professionals.* January 2011.

3   US Department of Health, Education, and Welfare. "Vital Statistics of the United States, 1970 Volume II–Section 5 Life Tables," Public Health Service, Health Resources Administration, National Center for Health Statistics.

What Types of Women Would Benefit Most from Reading This Book?

Personally, we think it's the responsibility of all women to read this book. Whether you're married or single, divorced or widowed, working full-time or part-time, a professional or stay-at-home mom, ready for retirement or just beginning your career, *Women & Retirement Planning: Understanding Retirement Plans, Investment Choices, and Retirement Plan Distributions* is for you. If you wish to take responsibility for your retirement, this book offers a terrific starting point.

There are books in the marketplace that talk about retirement. Some books even mention the IRA, or the 401(k), or other plan. However, the devil is in the details. It's crucial to know the details of any and all plans in which you're participating or are considering participating. Even if you access the Internet and spend countless hours seeking the kind of information that's in these pages, you may not be successful.

The purpose of this book is to allow you to develop a basic understanding about retirement. We attempt to crystallize the main features of all available retirement plans, including contribution limits and deadlines for such contributions. We then go through an extended discussion of mutual funds. This includes a description of all the types of mutual funds that are available, key factors to look at when selecting mutual funds, and a discussion about asset allocation. Why does the book spend three chapters on mutual funds? Because they are presently the most widely used investment vehicle inside these retirement plans. However, for those who are more adventurous, we offer an overview of other possible investment choices. After the discussion of mutual funds, we get to the heart and thesis of the book. We discuss the distribution rules for each retirement plan. This is followed by a discussion of distributions necessitated by the death of the account owner. And finally, we top things off with an introduction to several often-used distribution strategies.

Take a moment; peruse the contents. We believe that you'll be happy with the manner in which the book is written and with the information that can help with your decision making. So take that step that will make your efforts toward securing a better retirement a little easier.

CHAPTER 1:
RETIREMENT PLANS THAT YOU MAY HAVE

Like most of us, you're probably planning to provide for at least a portion of your retirement income from investments you've made to an IRA, from a company-sponsored retirement plan, or both. Many kinds of plans exist, all designed to help you save for retirement.

In this chapter, we present an overview of common retirement plans. Essentially, this chapter establishes a baseline of information from which you may identify the types of plans in which you currently participate or that you might want to consider for future participation. So sit back and enjoy the read. It should be very educational.

Retirement plans can be Individual Retirement Arrangements (IRAs), defined contribution plans, or defined benefit plans.

There are many types of IRAs; some you can establish for yourself, while others must be set up by your employer. With an IRA, the amount available at retirement depends on both the level of funding and the performance of the invested funds.

Defined contribution plans are employer-sponsored retirement plans that do not promise a specific amount of benefit at retirement. Instead, employees or their employer contribute to employees' accounts under the plan, sometimes at a set rate (such as 5 percent of compensation annually). These accounts can either be trustee directed, meaning the employer or its representative chooses the investment allocations, or individually directed by the employee. The plan can also be pooled, meaning that all plan money is combined and managed together, or segregated, where the individual employee accounts are established and directed by each employee. At retirement, an employee receives the accumulated contributions, plus earnings or minus losses, on the invested amounts.[4]

Below are types of employer-sponsored defined contribution retirement plans:
- profit-sharing plans
- money purchase pension plans
- target benefit plans
- thrift savings plans
- stock bonus
- employer stock ownership plans (ESOPs)
- 401(k)

Defined benefit plans, unlike defined contribution plans, promise a specified benefit at retirement based on salary earned throughout years of employment and number of years of service. Employer contributions must be sufficient to fund promised benefits.[5] Unlike the defined contribution plans, where earnings and losses affect the benefits payable to the individual, the defined benefit plan guarantees an annual benefit to the retired employee. The benefits are calculated by an actuary and formalized in the plan document. The plan allows employees to earn benefits as soon as they become participants; however, the right to secure a minimum benefit is usually based on the number of years worked.[6] Defined benefit plans are always pooled accounts, although each individual gets a report at the end of the year specifying his or her anticipated benefits.

Types of defined benefit plans include:
- defined benefit;
- cash balance; and
- fully funded and insured 412(i) and 412(e).

The next sections explore three categories of plans: IRAs, employer-funded plans, and employee-funded plans.

---

4   "Choosing a Retirement Solution for Your Small Business." *IRS Publication 3998*. p. 3.
5   Ibid.
6   Krass, Stephen J. *Pension Answer Book*. Fredrick, MD: Aspen Publishers, 2011. p. 2.

Individual Retirement Arrangements (IRAs)	Employer Funded	Employee Funded
Traditional IRA	SEP IRA	SIMPLE IRA
Roth IRA	Profit sharing	SARSEP
	Money purchase	401(k)
	Defined benefit .	403(b)
	Cash balance	457(b)
	412(e)	

IRAs

An IRA may be a traditional IRA or a Roth IRA. This section defines each type and explains the differences.

Traditional IRA

A traditional IRA is an account set up with a financial institution such as a bank, brokerage firm, insurance company, or mutual fund company. The sole purpose of the account is to store funds that are intended to be used during the account owner's retirement. A traditional IRA is used to hold investments as well as any capital gains, dividends, and interest that such investments may generate, on a tax-deferred basis. Tax-deferred means you don't pay the taxes at the time you make the investment or earn the dividends; taxes are paid upon a future event, such as when money is taken from the account.

Many types of investments may be used to fund an IRA: stocks, bonds, mutual funds, annuities, certificates of deposit, etc. At the same time, there are specific investments that cannot be used to fund an IRA: life insurance and collectibles are two examples.

In order to establish and make current-year contributions to a traditional IRA, you must meet two criteria: (1) the account owner must have earned income; and (2) the account owner must be younger than age 70 ½ during the year of contribution. Earned income is reported on a W-2 from an employer; it can also be income from self-employment. Individuals under the age of eighteen can establish a traditional IRA account as long as they have earned income; however, the financial institution where the traditional IRA has been set up may require a legal guardian to transact business on behalf of the minor because contract law prohibits a minor from entering into a binding legal contract.

Money can also be moved into an IRA by an individual who does not have current income. For example, after separation from employment, you might move money accumulated in an employer retirement plan to an IRA; this is referred to as a rollover IRA. Contributions to a rollover IRA can be made at any time and do not require earned income, since the contributions were made out of income earned in previous years. Another way money is placed into a traditional IRA is through a process called recharacterization. A recharacterization occurs when money originally contributed to a Roth IRA needs to be removed because of earned-income limitations. A recharacterization can also reverse a taxable conversion, changing the account back to a traditional IRA from a Roth IRA.

Traditional IRA contributions are made using after-tax dollars, and therefore may be partially or fully tax deductible for federal income tax purposes. But beware; if you withdraw money from an IRA before you reach age 59 ½, you will pay an early withdrawal penalty of 10 percent. Most IRA distributions are taxed as ordinary income, the exception being the portion representing any nondeductible contributions. Nondeductible contributions occur when either by account-owner choice or IRS limitation, an income tax deduction is not taken during the year of the contribution. And you must begin to take traditional IRA distributions by age 70 ½, or you may be penalized 50 percent on any required amount not withdrawn.

Roth IRA

Like the traditional IRA, the Roth IRA is an account that is used to house funds that are intended to be used during the account owner's retirement. Investments, capital gains, dividends, and interest in a Roth IRA are not subject to tax while they remain in the account. More importantly, unlike the traditional IRA, where distributions are subject to federal and possibly state income tax, distributions from a Roth IRA are tax-free! Yes, tax-free—as long as certain criteria are met prior to distribution. (These requirements will be discussed in chapter 7.)

As with the traditional IRA, the Roth account must be established through and held by a third-party custodian. Similarly, in order to establish and contribute to a Roth IRA account, the account owner must have earnings from an employer or self-employment. However, there are income limitations that cannot be exceeded in order to make a Roth IRA contribution. Unlike the traditional IRA, the account owner can contribute to a Roth IRA after reaching age 70 ½, as long as he or she has earnings from employment. Like the traditional IRA, individuals under the age of eighteen can contribute to a Roth IRA, as long as they have earnings from employment. Again, like the traditional IRA, there may be requirements for a legal guardian or court-appointed individual to transact business on behalf of a minor.

Investments are made with after-tax dollars but are not federally tax deductible, which allows withdrawals to be tax-free. And as important, and unlike with traditional IRAs, account owners are not required to take distributions by age 70 ½—or ever. But withdrawals of earnings prior to age 59 ½ may be subject to a 10 percent early withdrawal penalty unless certain criteria are met.

Five differences between the traditional IRA and the Roth IRA are:
1. Tax deductibility of contributions:
   - The traditional IRA contribution may be deductible for tax purposes.
   - The Roth IRA contribution is not tax deductible.
2. Age limitation:
   - To make a traditional IRA contribution, you cannot be age 70 ½ or older in the year of the contribution.
   - The Roth IRA allows anyone with earnings to make a contribution, regardless of age.
3. Distributions:
   - In a traditional IRA, distributions must begin by age 70 ½.
   - There is no requirement to take distributions from a Roth IRA starting at age 70 ½.
4. Taxability of distributions:
   - Distributions from a traditional IRA are subject to federal and state income tax.
   - Distributions from a Roth IRA are tax-free if certain criteria are met.
5. Contribution income limitations:
   - There are no income limits restricting the amount of contribution to a traditional IRA.
   - Income limits restrict contributions to Roth IRAs.

The following types of IRAs are variations of the traditional IRA and Roth IRA;

the underlying account is either a traditional IRA or a Roth IRA. Let's take a closer look at these account titles:

- Roth conversion
- beneficiary IRA
- spousal IRA
- payroll deducted IRA
- rollover IRA

Roth Conversion

A Roth conversion is a type of Roth IRA account that was previously a traditional IRA or an employer retirement plan. The money in the account was taxed and redesignated a Roth IRA, so future distributions would be tax-free. Roth conversion accounts do not need to be kept separate from contributory Roth IRA accounts. If you have separate Roth IRA accounts and conversion accounts, you might consider consolidating the accounts if you are being charged annual trustee fees for both accounts.

Beneficiary IRA

A beneficiary IRA is sometimes known as an Inherited IRA, a Stretch IRA, or a Beneficiary Designated Account (BDA). The beneficiary IRA is a retirement account that is inherited from another individual. The beneficiary IRA can be either a traditional IRA or a Roth IRA. The beneficiary IRA allows the account to continue to grow tax-deferred.

Since this is a traditional or Roth IRA, the beneficiary IRA is an account used to hold investments, plus any capital gains, dividends, and interest that such investments may generate, on a tax-deferred basis. This means that all investments, gains, dividends, and interest are not subject to tax while they remain in the beneficiary IRA. These investments can be varied and can include stocks, bonds, mutual funds, certificates of deposit, etc.

This type of account is opened when an account owner passes away and leaves a retirement account to a designated beneficiary. If the beneficiary is someone other than the surviving spouse, assets cannot be transferred to an existing or new IRA owned by the beneficiary; they must be transferred to an account that includes the original owner's name and "for the benefit of" the named beneficiary. A common registration would read: "Natalie Smith beneficiary of John Smith IRA" or "John Smith IRA fbo (for benefit of) Natalie Smith."

Again, since this is a traditional or Roth IRA, the beneficiary IRA account must be established through and held by a third-party custodian. But unlike the traditional and Roth IRA, contributions generally cannot be made to the beneficiary IRA. Only a surviving spouse has the ability to make contributions to a beneficiary IRA account.

Another way for a beneficiary IRA to receive money is from an employer-sponsored retirement plan: 401(k), profit sharing, defined benefit, etc. The employer's plan must contain language allowing for a beneficiary to move money directly to a beneficiary IRA or convert directly from the employer's retirement plan to a beneficiary Roth IRA. Funds converted directly from the employer's retirement plan to a beneficiary Roth IRA are taxable to the beneficiary.

Money cannot be held in a beneficiary IRA indefinitely. Distributions must begin to the beneficiary within a specified time frame, depending on the age of the account owner and the type of account owned at the time of his or her passing. The distribution rules are complex, and a financial advisor or tax professional should be consulted. The beneficiary may be able to take distributions from the account over his or her single life expectancy or take distributions so that the entire balance is withdrawn within five years. These rules are referred to as Required Minimum Distributions or Minimum Required Distributions, which direct the beneficiary to start taking distributions to avoid a 50 percent penalty for not taking the distributions timely. The IRS requires a minimum distribution, but the account holder can take more than the required minimum. An entire chapter, chapter 7, is devoted to retirement plan distributions.

Spousal IRA

The spousal IRA is either a traditional IRA or a Roth IRA. The spousal IRA is a term used to describe the situation that occurs when a spouse does not have earnings; the non–wage-earning spouse can make contributions based on his or her spouse's earnings. For example: Jane earned $62,000; however, her husband's business, a sole proprietorship, generated a loss. Jane's husband can still make an IRA contribution based on Jane's earnings. Another situation when a spousal IRA might be used is when the wage-earner is over age 70 ½ and no longer allowed to make a traditional IRA contribution. A younger spouse (under 70 ½) who doesn't have earnings can still contribute to an IRA, since he or she still qualifies for a traditional IRA contribution.

Payroll Deducted IRA

A payroll deducted IRA is either a traditional or Roth IRA, but the contributions are made by an employer. The employer makes payments to the IRA instead of paying the employee that amount in salary or wages. The payments to the IRA are treated as if they were part of the employee's pay—that is, payroll taxes are withheld on the amount. If the contribution is made to a traditional IRA, the employee may be able to deduct the contribution on his or her federal income tax return. If the contribution is made to a Roth IRA, the contribution is not deductible on a federal income tax return.

Rollover IRA

"Rollover" is not a type of IRA; it is a title used to distinguish traditional IRAs that originate from an employer retirement plan. In the past, money from these plans was kept separate from other contributory IRAs so that they could be rolled into another employer's retirement plan in order to receive special tax treatment when the account owner retires and withdraws funds from the retirement plan. The rules have changed, though, and these rollover amounts no longer need to be segregated from contributory or other pre-tax contributions; the rollover amounts can be rolled to other IRAs or to other qualified plans. The special tax savings, for the most part, have been phased out.

Employer-Funded Retirement Plans

As a way to encourage people to save for retirement, employers are offered tax incentives for making contributions on behalf of their employees or establishing plans where employees can save for their own retirement.

Employer-funded retirement plans are plans where your employer makes plan contributions for you, the employee. These plans do not allow employees to make contributions from salary deferrals. These plans can receive rollover money from IRAs as well as from other employer-sponsored retirement plans, such as SEP IRAs, 401(k)s, etc.—as long as the plan document has this provision.

Simplified Employee Pension or SEP IRA

A SEP IRA is an IRA where the employer must contribute a uniform percentage of pay for each eligible employee. The employer is not required to make contributions every year, though.[7] In a year where a contribution is made for one employee, all eligible employees must receive a contribution. Since these accounts are IRA accounts, each

---

7   "Choosing a Retirement Solution for Your Small Business." *IRS Publication 3998.* p. 6.

individual has his or her own account: the individual employee controls the investment direction and distributions.

Like the traditional IRA, the SEP IRA is an account used to hold investments intended to be used during the account owner's retirement. Any capital gains, dividends, and interest that such investments may generate are tax-deferred until withdrawn. All investments, gains, dividends, and interest are not subject to tax while they remain in the SEP IRA. These investments can be varied and can include stocks, bonds, mutual funds, certificates of deposit, etc.

As with a traditional IRA, the SEP IRA account must be established through and held by a third-party custodian. In order for an employee to receive a contribution to the SEP IRA account, the employee must have earnings in the form of a W-2. Business owners are generally treated as employees and can have contributions made to their SEP IRA accounts, as long as the business owner receives a W-2 or has earned income from self-employment.

Unlike a traditional IRA, contributions can be made to a SEP IRA even after the employee or business owner has reached age 70 ½, as long as he or she has earnings from employment. Individuals under the age of eighteen are generally excluded from the plan. We'll discuss eligibility in more detail in chapter 2. However, the employer can elect to cover minors under the plan. Again, like the traditional IRA, check with the custodian to determine their requirements for a legal guardian or court-appointed individual to transact business on behalf of the minor.

The employer contribution is not federally taxed when contributed, but it is taxed when the money is withdrawn. Distributions may be subject to state income tax as well as federal. The individual does not receive a tax deduction for the employer contributions to the plan; the business receives the tax deduction for all contributions. Contributions to the SEP account can be made up until the business tax return is filed, including extensions.

Once money is contributed to a SEP IRA by your employer, it belongs to you. You can withdraw the contributions and any associated earnings from the account at any time for any reason. Just like the traditional IRA, money should not be withdrawn from the account before you reach age 59 ½, though, due to the 10 percent early withdrawal penalty. The distributions are taxed as ordinary income. And, like the traditional IRA, withdrawals must begin by age 70 ½ or you may be penalized 50 percent for not withdrawing enough money.

Profit-Sharing Plan

A profit-sharing plan is a defined contribution plan. This plan is more complex than the SEP IRA. The plan holds the money in a trust account until one of the following occurs:

1. You leave employment.
2. You retire.
3. You become disabled.
4. You pass away.

In the past, employers made contributions to profit-sharing plans when the company had reached stated profitability goals. This profitability requirement is no longer mandatory. Most profit-sharing plan contributions are based on a percentage of pay. These accounts can be pooled or segregated, trustee- or individually directed. The plan document and/ or the Summary Plan Description will provide additional information on whether the individual employee or the employer's representative is directing the investments and whether the accounts are being managed as a pooled investment. The individual receives an annual statement showing gains and losses in the account as well as annual employer contributions made to the account. Since this is a defined contribution plan, the amount of money available at retirement is not guaranteed; the balance available at retirement is subject to market fluctuations. Like the SEP IRA, annual contributions by the employer are voluntary. If the employer makes contributions for any eligible employee, other eligible employees must also receive a contribution. The employer decides if a contribution is going to be made. The contribution can be made to the employee's account up until the company's tax return is filed, including extensions.

Like the SEP IRA, the profit-sharing plan
- holds investments intended to be used during the account owner's retirement;
- retains capital gains, dividends, and interest on a tax-deferred basis until withdrawn;
- holds investments that can include stocks, bonds, mutual funds, certificates of deposit, etc.;
- requires that employees must have earnings in the form of W-2 or the business owner has earned income from self-employment in order to receive a contribution to the plan;
- requires that employers make contributions to all eligible employees,

including those who are age 70 ½ or older (employees who are under the age of twenty-one may be excluded from receiving plan contributions);

- contributes money on a pre-tax basis, meaning the business receives the tax deduction for all contributions;
- discourages any withdrawals from the account prior to attaining age 59 ½ due to the 10 percent early withdrawal penalty; and
- distributions are taxed as ordinary income.

Unlike the SEP IRA, the plan trustee can be an individual and is commonly the business owner. The employer could hire an outside company, such as a bank or insurance company, to act as trustee.

Some companies may require distributions starting at normal retirement age, as defined in the plan document, but tax law allows employees to delay taking distributions from the accounts after attaining age 70 ½ if they are still employed and if the plan document allows. Anyone who owns 5 percent or more of the company and their family members cannot delay distributions after attaining age 70 ½.

Variations of the profit-sharing plan are:

- Keogh or HR 10: a profit-sharing or money purchase pension plan that is established by a self-employed business, which is either a partnership or sole proprietorship
- Stock bonus plan: a profit-sharing or money purchase pension plan that is funded using employer stock

Money Purchase Pension Plan

The money purchase pension plan is a defined contribution plan. Like the profit-sharing plan, the plan's money is held in a trust account for the plan until one of the four actions noted in the profit-sharing plan discussion—the person leaves employment, retires, becomes disabled or passes away—occurs. These accounts can be pooled or segregated; they may also be trustee- or individually directed. The plan document and/or the Summary Plan Description will provide additional information on whether the individual employee or the employer representative is directing the investments and whether the accounts are being managed as a pooled investment. The individual will receive an annual statement showing gains and losses in the account as well as annual employer contribution information. Since this is a defined contribution plan, the amount of money available at retirement is not guaranteed: the balance available at retirement is subject to market fluctuations.

This plan differs from the profit-sharing plan because the employer must contribute a specified amount, which is listed in the plan document (again, usually a percentage of pay). Because this type of plan requires an annual employer contribution, it isn't as popular as the profit-sharing plan. The money purchase pension plan has additional requirements that cause these plans to be more complex than the profit-sharing plan.

Variations of the money purchase pension plan are:

- Keogh or HR 10: a profit-sharing or money purchase pension plan that is established by a self-employed business that is either a partnership or sole proprietorship
- Stock bonus plan: a profit-sharing or money purchase pension plan that is funded using employer stock

Target Benefit Plan

A target benefit plan is a defined contribution plan. This is a pension plan that combines the characteristics of the money purchase plan with those of a defined benefit plan. Like the money purchase plan, the target benefit plan has a stated amount that must be funded annually. The plan's funding level is based on a stated benefit formula, like the defined benefit plan. However, the target benefit is not as complex as the defined benefit plan. Once the funding amount is identified, the plan no longer requires annual certification by an actuary. Like the money purchase plan, the contribution is limited to a percentage of pay. Assets available at retirement are not guaranteed; the account value is subject to market fluctuations. This plan type is not common. Defined benefit plans and cash balance plans are more common.

Defined Benefit Plan

A defined benefit, also known as the traditional pension plan, promises the participant a specified monthly benefit at retirement. Often, the benefit is based on factors such as salary, age, and the number of years worked for the employer.[8] Like the money purchase plan, this plan requires the employer to make annual contributions, and the money is held in a trust account. This plan does not allow individual investment direction; it is a trustee-directed, pooled account. The contribution formula provides a larger guaranteed benefit to employees who are closer to retirement age and who have

---

8   "Choosing a Retirement Solution for Your Small Business." *IRS Publication 3998. p. 3.*

worked longer. So this plan favors older employees and owners who may not have saved earlier in their working careers. The contribution formula is written in the plan document when the plan is established. Annually, an actuary compares actual results with expected results to determine the amount of contribution.

Like the profit-sharing plan, the defined benefit plan
- holds investments intended to be used during the account owner's retirement;
- retains capital gains, dividends, and interest on a tax-deferred basis until withdrawn;
- holds investments that can include stocks, bonds, mutual funds, certificates of deposit, etc.;
- requires that employees must have earnings in the form of W-2 or that the business owner has earned income from self-employment in order to receive a contribution to the plan;
- requires the employer to make contributions on behalf of all eligible employees, including those who are 70 ½ or older. Employees who are under age twenty-one may be excluded from the plan;
- contributes money on a pre-tax basis, meaning that the business receives the tax deduction for all contributions; and
- distributions are taxed as ordinary income.

The plan trustee can be an individual and is commonly the business owner. The employer could hire an outside company to act as trustee, like a bank or insurance company.

Some companies may require distributions starting at normal retirement age as defined in the plan document, but tax law allows employees to delay taking distributions from the accounts after attaining age 70 ½ if still employed and if the plan document allows. Anyone who owns 5 percent or more of the company, or their family members, cannot delay distributions after attaining age 70 ½.

As a general rule, money should not be withdrawn from the account prior to attaining age 59 ½, due to the 10 percent early withdrawal penalty. Check with the plan administrator for specific requirements.

Some defined benefit plans don't allow distributions until age 65 or normal retirement age, as specified in the plan document.

Cash Balance Plan

A cash balance plan is a type of defined benefit plan that includes some elements that are similar to a money purchase pension plan:

- The benefit amount is computed based on a formula using contribution and earning credits.
- Each participant has a hypothetical account.[9]
- It requires the employer to designate a contribution formula that must be funded annually.
- The money is held in a trust account.

The contribution formula is based on the age of the employees and length of service, in addition to compensation. Due to the high cost of maintaining a defined benefit plan, larger employers are terminating their defined benefit plans in favor of cash balance plans. Employers find that cash balance plans are less complicated and easier to explain to employees. Also, cash balance plans may provide greater benefits to younger employees than the traditional defined benefit plans.

Fully Insured Defined Benefit Plans: 412(e) Plan

This is a variation of the defined benefit plan. It is funded through the use of insurance policies and annuities. These plans have garnered the attention of the IRS and are not as popular with employers. These plans may also be known by their former name: 412(i). The "412" refers to the Internal Revenue Code section that contains the laws that define this plan. This plan does not need an annual actuarial certification, like defined benefit or cash balance plans. This plan requires insurability of the individual(s) covered under the plan.

In summary, there are three types of defined benefit plans:

- traditional defined benefit
- cash balance
- fully insured defined benefit plans: 412(e)

---

9   "Choosing a Retirement Solution for Your Small Business." *IRS Publication 3998.* p. 3.

Employee-Funded Retirement Plans (Salary Deferral Plans)

Some employers want their employees to help fund their individual retirement plans. Instead of the employer making all of the contributions to the plan, these plan types allow the employee to make contributions directly from their wages or salary. These plans are referred to as salary deferral retirement plans, because the individual has the ability to take the cash or defer the payment of wages to a future date. The deferrals an employee makes are subject to Social Security and Medicare taxes, but they are not subject to federal income tax. Depending on your state of residency, the salary deferrals could be subject to state income taxes.

SIMPLE IRA

SIMPLE is an acronym for Savings Incentive Match Plan for Employees. The employer makes contributions to an IRA account on behalf of employees, allowing each individual to have his or her own account. Each individual employee controls the investment direction and distributions.

With this arrangement, the employees direct the employer as to how much to take from their salary for the contribution. The employer must make a contribution, either as a matching contribution or as a non-elective contribution, where all eligible employees will receive an employer contribution whether or not they are making a salary deferral. The employer must elect prior to the beginning of the year whether the plan will provide a match or the non-elective contribution.

The match is contingent upon the employee making a salary deferral; it is also limited to the lesser of 3 percent of annual salary or the amount the employee contributes. For example, if the employee contributes 5 percent of her paycheck, the employer will match up to 3 percent of her annual salary. It may be best to explain this with an example: Julie earns $20,000 annually and decides to start deferring $10 per month from her pay, for a total of $120 for the year. The employer must match Julie's salary deferral by contributing $120 to Julie's SIMPLE IRA. However, if Julie deferred $100 per month from her pay, for a total of $1,200 for the year, the employer would only match the first $600 (3 percent of $20,000, her annual compensation).

The non-elective contribution is limited to 2 percent of annual salary. This alternative is not as popular with employers as the matching contribution. Unlike the matching contribution, where only those employees electing a salary deferral will receive an employer contribution, all eligible employees will receive contributions equal to 2 percent of their pay.

There are complex rules that must be followed by both the employee and employer when contributing to this plan; a financial advisor or tax professional should be consulted. This plan is only available to employers with fewer than a hundred employees who earned $5,000 or more the previous tax year.

Like the traditional IRA, the SIMPLE IRA:

- holds investments intended to be used during the account owner's retirement;
- retains capital gains, dividends, and interest on a tax-deferred basis until withdrawn;
- holds investments that can include stocks, bonds, mutual funds, certificates of deposit, etc;
- requires that employees must have earnings in the form of W-2 or that the business owner has earned income from self-employment in order to receive a contribution to the plan;
- requires the employer to make contributions to all eligible employees including those who are age 70 ½ or older;
- contributes money on a pre-tax basis, meaning the business receives the tax deduction for all contributions;
- discourages any withdrawals from the account prior to attaining age 59 ½ due to the 10 percent early withdrawal penalty; and
- distributions are taxed as ordinary income.

Plan assets are held by a third-party custodian, which can be a brokerage firm, mutual fund company, bank, or insurance company. Employees must start distributions from the accounts after attaining age 70 ½ or they may be penalized 50 percent for not withdrawing enough money.

Because the SIMPLE IRA is an employer-sponsored retirement plan, the employee can continue to make salary deferral contributions after attaining age 70 ½ if he or she is still employed. Another difference pertains to the early withdrawal penalty. If the individual removes money from the SIMPLE IRA within two years of the initial deposit, a 25 percent penalty will be assessed if the employee is under age 59 ½. The 25 percent early withdrawal penalty drops to 10 percent after the two-year holding period has been met. Even though the employee makes a salary deferral, the entire contribution to the plan is deductible by the employer, not the individual.

SARSEP

The SARSEP is a salary deferral SEP plan. As the employee, you elect to have money withheld from your salary and contributed to a traditional IRA account; each individual will have his or her own account and will control the investment direction and distributions. The employer can also contribute to the plan. The SARSEP is only available to employers with fewer than twenty-five eligible employees.

Although these plans were intended to be a simplified version of a 401(k) plan for smaller employers, the IRS realized, through plan audits, that employers didn't understand the rules and were violating the provisions of the plans. In 1997, when the SIMPLE IRA became available, the SARSEP was no longer allowed to be established. An employer with an existing SARSEP can continue to fund the plan, but new plans can no longer be established.

Traditional 401(k) Plan

The traditional 401(k) plan is a defined contribution plan. This is a retirement plan funded by employee pre-tax or designated Roth after-tax contributions, which may include an employer's match and/or profit-sharing contribution. This plan is a type of profit-sharing plan; therefore, it follows the profit-sharing rules. Typically, plan contributions are invested in a selection of mutual funds. These accounts are typically individually directed using segregated accounts, which means each individual has a separate account.

Earnings and losses on the investments impact the total amount available for distribution. The account values are not guaranteed. Many large employers offer traditional 401(k)s to remain competitive in an attempt to retain and attract employees.

There are three discrimination tests that traditional 401(k) plans must pass on an annual basis. These tests ensure that the owners and highly compensated employees who are able to make higher contributions, because of their higher salaries, are limited in their ability to make deferrals. By definition, highly compensated employees are individuals who own 5 percent or more of the business, family members, and other individuals earning more than $115,000 annually. This annual earnings limit, $115,000, is indexed for inflation and reflects the 2013 annual limit. These highly compensated employees are restricted in their contributions relative to the contributions made by the non-highly compensated employees.

A very simplified example of one of the discrimination tests is limiting highly compensated individuals to a salary deferral of only 2 percent more than the non-highly compensated employees' average deferral percentage. For example, if the non-highly compensated, as a group, defer on average 5 percent of their pay, the highly compensated employees are limited to a 7 percent average salary deferral. An owner earning $100,000 would only be able to defer $7,000, instead of the current annual limit of $17,500 (2013 deferral limit). The discrimination tests are complex and are performed annually by the plan administrator. If the discrimination tests are not passed, the contributions for the highly compensated can be reduced or eliminated, or the employer may need to make additional contributions to correct the deficiency. One way to simplify the annual requirements is to establish a Safe Harbor 401(k) plan, which is discussed next.

Safe Harbor 401(k) Plan

The Safe Harbor 401(k) is a variation of the 401(k) plan. According to IRS Publication 3998, *Choosing a Retirement Solution for Your Small Business*, "a Safe Harbor 401(k) plan is intended to encourage plan participation among rank-and-file employees and to ease administrative burden by eliminating the tests applied under a traditional 401(k) plan. This plan is ideal for businesses with highly compensated employees whose contributions would be limited in a traditional 401(k) plan."[10] These plans usually provide individual accounts for each of the plan participants and are individually directed. Some employers will design the plan with pooled investments and trustee direction instead of individual direction. This is a plan design feature that is decided when the plan is established.

Like the SIMPLE IRA, but unlike the traditional 401(k), the employer is required to either make a matching contribution or a non-elective contribution for all eligible employees, whether or not they are making a salary deferral. If you ever received a letter from your employer stating that the discrimination test was not met by the 401(k), and you were required to report a portion of your salary deferral on your tax return as earnings, you have firsthand experience with discrimination testing. Discrimination testing is not required in the Safe Harbor 401(k). As long as the employer makes a contribution and provides notification prior to the beginning of the year, the possibility of having deferrals returned at the end of the year is eliminated. Since the Safe Harbor 401(k) is a type of 401(k) plan, the deferrals can be pre-tax or designated Roth after-tax contributions.

---

10 "Choosing a Retirement Solution for Your Small Business." *IRS Publication 3998*. p. 6.

403(b) or Tax-Sheltered Annuity (TSA) Plan

The 403(b) is a plan available to nonprofit organizations chartered under Internal Revenue Code section 501(c)(3). These organizations are typically nonprofit schools, hospitals, churches, or charitable agencies. The charter for the nonprofit organization specifies that the organization is a 501(c)(3).[11]

These plan contributions can be invested in mutual funds or annuities. These accounts are typically individually directed using segregated accounts, which means each individual will have a separate account. Like the traditional 401(k) plan, this plan can have pre-tax or designated Roth after-tax deferrals. The plans may include employer matching or discretionary contributions, but employer contributions are not common.

The 403(b) has the following characteristics:

- holds investments intended to be used during the account owner's retirement;
- retains capital gains, dividends, and interest on a tax-deferred basis until withdrawn;
- holds investments that can only include mutual funds or annuities;
- requires that employees must have earnings in the form of W-2 in order to make a contribution to the plan (since the employers are chartered as nonprofit entities, self-employed businesses will not be able to establish a 403(b));
- must allow all eligible employees, including those who are 70 ½ or older, to make salary deferrals;
- contributes money on a pre-tax basis, meaning the employer receives the tax deduction for all contributions;
- discourages any withdrawals from the account prior to attaining age 59 ½ due to the 10 percent early withdrawal penalty; and
- distributions are taxed as ordinary income.

Many employers hire an outside company to act as trustee, like a bank or insurance company. Employees may delay taking distributions from the accounts after attaining age 70 ½ if still employed and if the plan document allows.

---

11   Krass, Stephen J. *Pension Answer Book.* Fredrick, MD: Aspen Publishers, 2011. p. 35–3.

457(b) Plan

The 457(b) is a type of deferred compensation plan. These plans are established by city, county, and state employers, but they also may be available to nonprofit organizations. Employers who usually offer 457(b) plans are city police departments and state universities. These plans are funded by employee salary deferrals.

The 457(b) has the following characteristics:

- holds investments intended to be used during the account owner's retirement;
- retains capital gains, dividends, and interest on a tax-deferred basis until withdrawn;
- holds investments that can include stocks, bonds, mutual funds or certificates of deposit, etc.;
- requires that employees must have earnings in the form of W-2 in order to make a contribution to the plan. (Since the employers are governmental or nonprofit entities, self-employed businesses will not be able to establish a 457(b));
- contributes money on a pre-tax basis, meaning the employer receives the tax deduction for all contributions;
- discourages any withdrawals from the account prior to attaining age 59 ½, due to the 10 percent early withdrawal penalty; and
- distributions are taxed as ordinary income.

Eligible employees, including those who are 70 ½ or older, can make salary deferrals. Employees who are under age twenty-one may be excluded from receiving plan contributions. Employees may delay taking distributions from the accounts after attaining age 70 ½ if still employed and if the plan document allows.

One unique feature of the 457(b) is that nonprofit organizations with a 457(b) plan are not able to roll over distributions to a traditional IRA. Employees of governmental entities, however, can roll over distributions to a traditional IRA.

Other Types of Retirement Plans

Employer Stock Ownership Plan ("ESOP")

This plan can be a profit-sharing plan, a 401(k), or a money purchase pension plan that is funded with employer stock instead of cash. Some 401(k) plans require the employer's matching contribution be made in employer stock.

Nonqualified Deferred Compensation Plan

Sometimes referred to as *top hat* or *golden handcuffs*, these plans could provide additional compensation incentives to salesmen, keep key employees motivated, help transition a business to a new owner, or help a restaurant chain get off the ground and on the map. This plan can be funded through salary deferral or by employer incentives. These arrangements come in many forms. We'll avoid detailing specifics, since nonqualified deferred compensation plans vary vastly in their terms. One thing that you need to know is that plan distributions cannot be rolled over to a traditional IRA or converted to a Roth IRA. Distributions will be taxed when paid or when the individual contract terms have been met.

Deferred Retirement Option Plans (DROP)

DROPs began in the early 1990s with public safety employees in Louisiana and spread quickly. DROPs were designed to increase total retirement benefits of state and local employees.[12] Employees who would otherwise be entitled to retire and receive benefits under the employer's defined benefit plan instead continue working. However, instead of having continued compensation and additional years of service taken into account for the defined benefit plan formula, the employee has a sum of money credited during each year of continued employment to a separate account under the employer's retirement plan.[13] In essence, the individual "retires" from the defined benefit plan and the employer instead makes payments to the DROP account. At retirement or separation from service, the individual will receive both the defined benefit payments in addition to a lump sum from the DROP plan.[14]

---

12   Perdue, Grady, PhD, CFP, and Joseph P. McCormack, PhD, CFA. "Don't Drop the Ball on Deferred Retirement Option Plans." *Journal of Financial Planning*, February 2000.

13   Calhoun, Carol V., and Arthur H. Tepler. "Deferred Retirement Option Plans (DROP Plans)." *Pension and Benefits Week*, October 13, 1998.

14   Deferred Retirement Option Programs. VanKampen. Seminar 2004.

PERS and TRS—Public Employee Retirement System and Teacher's Retirement System—are retirement plans of public employees and teachers. These plans are typically defined benefit plans sponsored by a state employer.

Thrift savings plans are profit-sharing or money purchase pension plans. The employee contributes a portion of pay, which the employer matches. The federal government offers a thrift savings plan to its employees that follows the 401(k) rules.

Summary

The following chart summarizes some of the key features of the plans discussed in this chapter. Only the main plan types have been included.

Feature	Traditional IRA	Roth IRA	SEP IRA	Profit Sharing	Defined Benefit	SIMPLE IRA	401(k)	403(b)
Invested in mutual funds, stocks, bonds, cds,	Yes	Yes	Yes	Yes	Yes	Yes	Yes	Mutual funds and annuities only
Established by	Individual	Individual	Employer	Employer	Employer	Employer	Employer	Employer
Individual or trustee directed investments	Individual	Individual	Individual	Trustee	Trustee	Individual	Usually individual	Usually individual
Pooled or Segregated accounts	Segregated	Segregated	Segregated	Usually Pooled	Pooled	Segregated	Usually Segregated	Usually Segregated
Tax deduction taken by	Individual; dependent upon income	No tax deduction available	Employer	Employer	Employer	Employer	Employer	Employer
Individual, employee or employer funded	Individual	Individual	Employer	Employer	Employer	Both	Both	Usually employee funded
After tax contributions	Yes	Yes	No	Check plan document	No	No	Yes, designated Roth	Yes, designated Roth
Early withdrawal penalty	Yes	Yes	Yes	Yes	Yes, if allowed; however plan may not allow early withdrawals	Yes	Yes	Yes
Required Minimum Distribution required	Yes	Not required during account owner's lifetime.	Yes	Yes, after separation from service and after age 70 ½.	Yes, after separation from service and after age 70 ½.	Yes	Yes, after separation from service and after age 70 ½.	Yes, after separation from service and after age 70 ½.
Distributions taxed as ordinary income	Yes	Generally not taxable	Yes	Yes	Yes	Yes	Yes	Yes
Accepts rollovers from IRA or other retirement plan	Yes	No, only from designated Roth 401(k) or 403(b)	Yes	Yes	Yes	No	Yes	Yes

CHAPTER 2:
CONTRIBUTION LIMITATIONS AND DEADLINES TO MAKE CONTRIBUTIONS

The many types of retirement plans can create confusion because each plan type has its own rules regarding timing and annual contribution limits. This chapter discusses the maximum contribution limitations and timing of such contributions for each of the retirement plans described in chapter 1.

IRAs

Traditional IRAs

The 2013 contribution limit for all IRAs—traditional, Roth, spousal, and payroll deduction—is the same. (The beneficiary IRA is not listed, since contributions cannot be made to the account by the beneficiary.) Individuals can contribute up to $5,500. If you have attained age 50, you are able to contribute an additional $1,000. The amount you can contribute is dependent upon your earned income and age.

Under age 50	Attained age 50
$5,500	$6,500

Betty is 72 years of age, and even though she has earned income, she cannot contribute to a traditional IRA because IRS regulations prohibit contributions the year in which Betty turns age 70 ½ and thereafter. Betty might, however, consider contributing to a Roth IRA, since there is no age limitation restricting her ability to contribute. Earned income is defined as either (W-2) wages from employment, or self-employment income. For example, if Betty earned $3,000 in 2013, she could contribute up to the amount she earned. She could make up to a $3,000 contribution to her Roth IRA. If, on the other hand, Betty earned $6,500 or more, she would be limited to contributing up to $6,500.

Roth IRA

As mentioned in chapter 1, the traditional IRA can be either tax-deductible or nondeductible. Deductibility does not limit the amount of the annual contribution. However, contributions to a Roth IRA, even though made with after-tax dollars, are not deductible on your tax return. Furthermore, your contributions may be limited by your level of income. The Roth IRA income limitations change annually. For 2013, the income limits are:

Single	Married Filing Joint	Married Filing Separate
$112,000 - $127,000	$178,000 - $188,000	$0 - $10,000

Karen is single and earns $45,000. Karen is below the income limitations for a Roth IRA. She can contribute up to $5,500; if she was age 50 or older, she could contribute up to $6,500. Now, let's say Karen's income increased to $115,000. According to the table above, she would not be able to contribute the maximum amount. She could, however, contribute up to $4,125. This is calculated in the following way:

$$(\$115,000-\$112,000) / (\$127,000-\$115,000)-1 \times \$5,500$$

The remainder of the $5,500, or $1,375, could be contributed to her traditional IRA, although it may not be deductible. Now, if Karen's income was $135,000, she would not be able to contribute to a Roth IRA, since her earnings exceed the maximum level of $127,000. For assistance in determining the precise amount that can be contributed, please refer to IRS Publication 590 or consult your tax professional.

Unlike qualified retirement plans, contributions cannot be made up until the extended tax-filing deadline. Traditional and Roth IRA contributions must be contributed by the tax-filing deadline for the year of the contribution. This is usually

April 15 of the year following the year for the contribution. The contribution must be postmarked to the IRA custodian no later than April 15 to meet the funding due date.

Employer-Funded Retirement Plans

All contributions made to an employer-funded retirement plan are deductible by the employer, on the business's federal income tax return. Contributions are not deductible by the individual employee.

Simplified Employee Pension or SEP IRA

The maximum contribution for 2013 that can be made to a SEP IRA is 25 percent of compensation, up to a maximum annual contribution of $51,000. An additional catch-up for individuals age 50 or older does not apply to employer-funded retirement plans.

> For example, Maxine earns $100,000. Her employer could contribute up to $25,000 to her SEP IRA account. If Maxine had earnings of $250,000, her employer could only contribute up to $51,000, even though the calculation shows $62,500 ($250,000 x 25 percent). The maximum contribution limit of $51,000 is attained when Maxine's compensation exceeds $204,000. One drawback to the SEP IRA is that the employer is not required to make annual contributions to the plan. The employer decides on a year-to-year basis whether to contribute to the SEP and how much to contribute.

> To be compliant with IRS regulations, the employer has up until the employer's tax-filing deadline, including extensions, to make and notify Maxine that a contribution has been made on her behalf.

Profit-Sharing Plan

The profit-sharing plan has the same contribution limit as the SEP IRA: 25 percent of compensation, up to $51,000. Again, this is the 2013 annual contribution limit; the catch-up for being age 50 or older does not apply to this plan. Also, similar to the SEP

IRA, the profit-sharing plan contributions can be made up until the employer's tax-filing deadline, including extensions.

Money Purchase Pension Plan

The money purchase pension plan has the same contribution limit as the SEP IRA and profit-sharing plan: 25 percent of compensation up to $51,000. This, too, is the 2013 annual contribution limit; similarly the catch-up for being age 50 or older does not apply. Like the SEP IRA and profit-sharing plan, money purchase contributions can be made up until the employer's tax-filing deadline, including extensions, but must be made by September 15 for calendar-year businesses.

Target Benefit Plan

The target benefit plan has the same contribution limit, age 50 catch-up restriction, and contribution-funding deadline as the previously mentioned plans.

Defined Benefit Plan

The defined benefit plan requires an actuary to calculate the annual employer-funding amount. The annual contribution is based on the ages and compensation of the employees eligible under the plan. The maximum benefit that can be used in the calculation is indexed annually for inflation, and therefore the annual funding changes from year to year. The maximum annual retirement benefit for 2013 is $205,000. However, the funding amounts vary from year to year as the actual experience of the plan is compared to the expected performance.

The actual experience can differ from the expected experience when: the investment performance differs from the plan assumptions; employees leave service earlier than expected; or new employees are hired. The plan contributions, like the money purchase plan, must be made by the employer's tax-filing deadline, including extensions, but cannot be made later than September 15 for calendar-year businesses.

Cash Balance Plan

Similar to the defined benefit plan, an actuary makes the annual employer-funding calculation. Also, like the defined benefit plan, the maximum annual retirement benefit is $205,000. The plan contributions must be made by the employer's tax-filing deadline, including extensions, but cannot be made later than September 15 for calendar-year businesses.

Fully Insured Defined Benefit Plans: 412(e) Plan

Like the cash balance plan, the 412(e) plan is a type of defined benefit plan. However, an actuary is not required to determine the annual employer-funding amount. The contributions are based on the insurance and annuity premiums, which are necessary to attain a desired retirement benefit. Once the desired funding amounts are identified, the premiums will not change from year to year.

Like the defined benefit plan and cash balance plan, the maximum retirement benefit is limited to $205,000 per year. The plan contributions must be made by the employer's tax-filing deadline, including extensions, but cannot be made later than September 15 for calendar-year businesses.

Employee-Funded Retirement Plans (Salary Deferral Plans)

Like employer-funded retirement plans, tax deductions are given to the employer for establishing the retirement plan for the business. Salary deferrals are subject to payroll taxes, Social Security, and Medicare withholding, but are not subject to federal withholding. Therefore, federal income tax is not withheld from the deferred amounts. State withholding may apply. The employer match, non-elective, top-heavy, or other type of employer contribution is not subject to payroll tax or federal income tax when contributed.

SIMPLE IRA

The SIMPLE IRA allows individuals to defer from salary up to 100 percent of earnings. The annual limit currently is $12,000 (2013 limit). An additional amount of $2,500 can be deferred for individuals age 50 or older. SIMPLE IRAs also have a mandatory employer contribution that is either a 3 percent match or a non-elective contribution of 2 percent of annual compensation. The 3 percent match is dollar-for-dollar up to 3 percent of compensation and is only granted to individuals who make a salary deferral to the SIMPLE IRA. Alternatively, the non-elective contribution is given to every eligible employee, regardless of whether the individual chooses to make a salary deferral under the retirement plan.

Let's look at two examples: Courtney participates in the SIMPLE IRA at her company and receives the employer's 3 percent matching contribution. Taylor does not participate in the SIMPLE IRA.

> Courtney's annual compensation is $50,000, and she defers $5,000 to the SIMPLE IRA. Courtney's employer matches her salary deferral by contributing an additional 3 percent of her $50,000 salary for a matching contribution of $1,500.

> Taylor, who earns $20,000, didn't make a salary deferral to the SIMPLE IRA. Taylor's employer would not make a matching contribution to Taylor's SIMPLE IRA account, since she did not participate by making a salary deferral to the plan.

However, if the employer had elected to opt for the non-elective contribution, 2 percent to all employees, Taylor would receive a $400 contribution to her SIMPLE IRA from the employer ($20,000 x 2 percent). Courtney would only receive $1,000 instead of $1,500 (2 percent of $50,000). The non-elective option is limited by the cap on compensation, which is $255,000 for 2013. The non-elective contribution *cannot* exceed $5,100 per individual, which is 2 percent of $255,000. By comparison, the 3 percent matching contribution is limited by the amount the individual defers from pay, up to the maximum deferral of $12,000.

> Let's look at another example. Lisa earns $500,000 annually. If her employer opted for the non-elective employer contribution, Lisa would receive an additional $5,100, whether or not she deferred $5,100 from her salary. If, instead, her employer opted to make a 3 percent matching employer contribution to all plan participants, Lisa would receive an additional $12,000 from her employer if she deferred $12,000 from her salary. If Lisa is over the age of 50, she could defer an additional $2,500, for a total deferral of $14,500. This additional deferral of $2,500 would also be matched by her employer. This would bring her total employer match to $14,500 also.

There are two deadlines to watch when working with employer contributions and employee salary deferrals. Any amount the employer contributes, whether match or non-elective, can be contributed by the employer up until the employer's tax-filing deadline, including extensions. Many employers choose to fund the employer-matching contribution at the same time the money is deferred from pay; however, this is not required. The employee salary deferrals must be deposited as soon as possible, according to the Department of Labor requirements. The IRS requires the salary-deferred money to be deposited no later than thirty days after the end of the month in which the money was withheld. As you will see with the other salary deferral types, the seven-day deposit requirement does not impact SIMPLE IRA deferrals.

SARSEP

Since 1997, SARSEPs can no longer be established. However, plans established prior to 1997 have been grandfathered, which means that they can continue to receive contributions. Contributions to a SARSEP can be a combination of employee salary deferral and employer contributions. The salary deferral is limited to $17,500, or $23,000 for individuals who are age 50 or older (2013 limits). If the employer elects to make a contribution to the SARSEP, it is made uniformly to all eligible employees. The employer can contribute up to 25 percent of compensation per individual. The combined annual limit of salary deferral and employer contribution cannot exceed $51,000 for employees under age 50, or $56,500 for individuals age 50 or older.

The salary deferral contribution must be made as soon as possible, per the Department of Labor guidelines that have been defined as within seven business days after being withheld from pay. Any employer contribution can be made up until the employer's tax filing, including extension.

Traditional 401(k) and Safe Harbor 401(k) Plans

The annual contribution limits for these 401(k) plans are the same as the SARSEP's annual limits. For 2013, annual salary deferral is limited to 100 percent of compensation, up to $17,500 for individuals under age 50, and $23,000 for individuals who are age 50 or older. The employer contribution can be up to 25 percent of compensation. The combined annual limit of salary deferral and employer contribution cannot exceed $51,000 for employees under age 50, or $56,500 for individuals age 50 or older. The plan document should be read to determine the annual limitation.

The difference between the traditional 401(k) and the Safe Harbor 401(k) is the discrimination testing. Refer to chapter 1 for an explanation of discrimination testing. The Safe Harbor 401(k) provides that, if the employer is willing to make a contribution for the employees, the complex discrimination testing is not necessary. This allows highly compensated employees to maximize their salary deferrals. (If the discrimination test is failed during the year, the highly compensated employees and owners may see a reduction in the form of a refund of deferred salary at the end of the year when the testing is completed.)

The traditional 401(k) does not require an employer contribution. However, some 401(k) plans limit the salary deferral to 25 percent of compensation. The Safe Harbor 401(k), like the SIMPLE IRA, requires an employer contribution to be either a matching contribution or a non-elective. Refer to your Summary Plan Description for specific plan limitations. A common match under the Safe Harbor 401(k) is 4 percent of compensation but can be as high as 6 percent of compensation.

The Department of Labor mandates employee deferrals must be deposited within seven business days after being withheld. Any employer contribution can be made up until the tax-filing deadline, including extension.

403(b) or Tax-Sheltered Annuity (TSA) Plan

The annual contribution limit to a 403(b) is the same as the 401(k): deferrals are limited to 100 percent of compensation, up to $17,500 or $23,000, based on age. Most 403(b)s only allow for salary deferrals, and the employer is not required to make contributions. However, if the employer elects to make a contribution, the contribution is limited to 25 percent of compensation, up to a total combined limit of $51,000, or $56,500 for those who are age 50 or older. The 403(b) also has an additional catch-up limit, which applies to individuals of teaching organizations who have worked for fifteen years or more with the same employer. This additional limit is $3,000 per year. Some teaching organizations, such as state universities, may also offer a 457(b) plan which, when combined with a 403(b), allows the annual deferral limit to apply to both plans, effectively allowing a deferral up to $35,000, or $46,000 for individuals who are age 50 or older. A discussion with your financial advisor or tax professional can determine if you qualify for the additional contribution and catch-up.

The Department of Labor mandates salary deferrals to be deposited within seven business days after being withheld. Any employer contribution can be made up until the tax-filing deadline, including extension.

457(b) Plan

The 457(b) plan is employee salary deferral only. The annual limit for salary deferral is 100 percent of compensation, up to $17,500, or $23,000 for individuals over age 50. The employer doesn't make contributions to this plan. When the employer offers both the 403(b) and 457(b) plans, the deferral limit can be doubled.

The Department of Labor mandates salary deferrals to be deposited within seven business days after being withheld. Any employer contribution can be made up until the tax-filing deadline, including extension.

Other Types of Retirement Plans

Employer Stock Ownership Plans (ESOP)

Contribution limits can vary from plan to plan. Some plans limit the ownership of the stock to current employees. Most plans will follow the annual funding limits outlined under profit-sharing and traditional 401(k) plans. The annual employer contribution can be up to 25 percent of compensation, plus the salary deferral component, up to $17,500, or $23,000 for those individuals age 50 or older. The total contribution, including the salary deferral and the employer contribution, cannot exceed $51,000 for someone under the age of 50, or $56,500 for someone over the age of 50. Trading restrictions on company stock may also limit the amount of individual contributions to the plan. Check with the plan administrator for information on your plan's specific restrictions.

The Department of Labor mandates salary deferrals to be deposited within seven business days after being withheld. Any employer contribution can be made up until the tax-filing deadline, including extension.

Nonqualified Deferred Compensation Plan

As defined in chapter 1, nonqualified deferred compensation plans provide additional incentives to critical employees, either through salary deferrals or employer bonuses. Nonqualified deferred compensation plans allow for contributions up to $1 million, based on reasonableness of compensation.

These plans are highly individualized and vary. Check with your employer on limitations and plan features. The plan may be designed for employer contributions, for employee salary deferrals, or a combination.

The Department of Labor guidelines do not impact this type of retirement plan. Since the contributions are nonqualified, the plan document should identify when contributions are due.

Summary

As we close this chapter, we include the following chart, which summarizes some of the key features of the plan types we've discussed.

Feature	Traditional IRA	Roth IRA	SEP	SIMPLE IRA	Profit Sharing	401(k)	403(b)	Defined Benefit
Annual Contribution	$5,500	$5,500	25% up to $51,000	$12,000	25% up to $51,000	$17,500	$17,500	Defined by plan, benefit not to exceed $205,000
Catch up for age 50 and over	$1,000	$1,000	Not Applicable	$2,500	Not Applicable	$5,500	$5,500	Not Applicable
Deadline for employee deferrals	Tax filing without extension	Tax filing without extension	Not Applicable	As soon as possible, not later than 30 days after month withheld.	Not Applicable	Deferrals within 7 business days, not later than 15 days after withheld.	Deferrals within 7 business days, not later than 15 days after withheld.	Not Applicable
Deadline for employer contributions	Individual's tax filing without extension	Individual's tax filing without extension	Employer's tax filing plus extension	Employer's tax filing plus extension	Employer's tax filing plus extension	Employer's tax filing plus extension	Employer's tax filing plus extension	Employer's tax filing plus extension

CHAPTER 3:
TYPES OF MUTUAL FUNDS

There is quite an array of mutual funds in the marketplace. They include everything from the very conservative money market fund, various types of bond funds, and all kinds of stock funds that include the higher-risk sector funds, such as commodities that may include gold, oil, futures, technology, and biotechnology funds.

Stock Mutual Funds

A stock mutual fund is generally one whose holdings are dominated by the common stock of various companies. A common stock is a security that represents ownership in a corporation. When delineated according to investment style, stock mutual funds are classified as value, growth, or blend. They can be further divided between domestic (US) and international funds. Mutual funds can be further grouped according to the size of companies owned. This is called "category." There are three categories of companies: large capitalization ("cap"), mid-cap, and small cap.

The market value or capitalization of a company is determined by multiplying the number of common shares of stock outstanding by the market price of a share of stock. Mutual funds are classified according to capitalization and fall into three categories:

Large Cap	Funds that hold a majority of companies that each have a capitalization of generally over $10 billion.
Mid-Cap	Funds that hold a majority of companies that each have a capitalization generally between $2 billion and $10 billion.
Small Cap	Funds that hold a majority of companies that each have a capitalization of under $2 billion.

There are three basic stock mutual fund investment styles:

Value	Typically contains holdings that have lower price to earnings and price to book value ratios in relation to growth funds. [The calculation of a company's price to earnings ratio is: market price per share/earnings per share.] Fund holdings may include companies that are not followed by the overall market and companies that are in turnaround situations (referred to as out-of-favor companies). Their holdings are generally reasonably priced and yet show characteristics of performance improvement.
Growth	Usually contains holdings that have higher price to earnings and price to book value ratios in relation to value funds. Fund holdings generally exhibit or are expected to exhibit accelerating earnings and market share growth (referred to as companies that are "in favor"). Such funds pursue capital appreciation; current income is either not considered or is a secondary issue.
Blend	Includes a combination of value and growth companies. In this category there are large cap, mid-cap, small cap, and international funds.

Bond Mutual Funds

Bond mutual funds have their primary (and possibly exclusive) holdings in debt securities of the US government and its agencies, in municipalities, in corporations, or in foreign governments. A bond or debt security is an IOU, a promise by the borrower to repay the lender on a certain date in the future the amount that was borrowed. During the life of the bond, the borrower promises to pay the lender a specific amount of interest periodically, usually semiannually, in exchange for the use of the money.

Bond funds are delineated based on style and creditworthiness of their holdings.

Style means the average life or duration of the bonds in the portfolio: short, intermediate, and long. The longer the average life or duration of bond holdings, the greater the bond fund's sensitivity to interest rate changes. (As interest rates rise, the underlying value of the bond holdings drops. Conversely, as interest rates drop, the underlying values of the bond holdings rise.)

Credit quality indicates how secure the companies are that have issued the bonds. They are broadly defined as: high (most secure), medium, and low. There is a further breakdown of credit rating: US government/agency has the highest overall credit rating and is the most secure; next is AAA, the highest credit rating for corporate bond issuers; and proceeding to holdings that are not rated and which are considered the riskiest.

Types of Mutual Funds

There are as many types of mutual funds in the marketplace as there are reasons or needs or desires for investing. The table below shows a general categorization of the variety of mutual funds available:

Money Market Funds	Contain short-term, high-quality securities that mainly provide safety of principal; the fund's current income is a secondary consideration (includes tax-free funds).
Short/Intermediate Bonds	Contain a mixture of U.S. government securities and credit-worthy corporate bonds that usually have an effective maturity and average duration or portfolio life typically between one to ten years.
Long-Term Bonds	Contain a variety of corporate bonds that emphasize credit-worthy companies and usually have an effective maturity greater than ten years (average duration or portfolio life could be less than ten years).
High-Yield Bonds	Include a range of higher yielding, lower rated corporate bonds (can include tax-free funds).
Municipal Bonds	Typically contain bond holdings of local governments and political subdivisions within a specific state (can be federal, state, and local tax free).
Balanced Funds	Contain a mixture of common stocks in addition to corporate, U.S. government and foreign bonds. These funds stress both current income and capital appreciation. The equity portion of this type of fund is generally in the large cap category and typically represents the majority of holdings.

Value Funds	Typically contain common stock holdings that have lower price to earnings and price to book value ratios in relation to growth funds. [The calculation of a company's price to earnings ratio is: market price per share divided by earnings per share.] Fund holdings may include companies that are not followed by the overall market and companies that are in turnaround situations. Their holdings are generally priced more reasonably and yet show characteristics of performance improvement. In this category there are large cap, mid-cap, small cap, and international funds.
Growth Funds	Usually contain common stock holdings that possess higher price to earnings and price to book value ratios in relation to value funds. Fund holdings generally exhibit or are expected to exhibit accelerated earnings and market share growth. Such funds pursue capital appreciation; current income is either not considered or is a secondary issue. In this category there are also large cap, mid-cap, small cap, and international funds.
Blend Funds	Include a combination of stock from both value and growth companies. In this category there are large cap, mid-cap, small cap, and international funds.
Sector/Country Funds	Include common stock of companies within the same industry or country; for example, energy, technology, biotechnology, gold, China, Japan, and Russia.
Domestic Funds	Include common stock of companies that are primarily in the United States.
International Funds	Include common stocks or bonds of companies that are in diverse markets and almost exclusively outside the United States.
Global Funds	Include stock or bonds of companies in diverse markets but can have significant holdings in U.S. companies.
Exchange Traded Funds	Commonly referred to as ETFs, these are a collection of common stocks or bonds that mirror the performance of a market index. ETFs cover all asset classes, such as U.S. large companies, small companies, overseas companies, etc. Unlike an index mutual fund, which is priced at the end of the day, the fund itself can be purchased or sold throughout the trading day. The stocks or bonds that make up the ETF do not change, regardless of how they're performing.

Index Mutual Funds	A collection of common stocks that mirrors the performance of a market index, that is, S&P 500. There are a limited number of indexes covered. Unlike the ETF, index funds can purchased or sold during the day, but will receive the end of the day price. The stocks or bonds that make up the index do not change regardless of how they're performing.
Target Date Funds	This type of fund is oftentimes referred to as life cycle or aged-based funds. These funds provide a portfolio of investments in stocks, bonds and cash. Periodically, it automatically resets its holdings based upon a date in the future (when usually a life-changing event is planned by the investor, i.e. retirement).
Asset Allocation Funds	Typically offers a portfolio that consists of stocks, bonds and cash. The allocation in the fund among asset classes depends on the objective of the fund. i.e., income, conservative growth, etc. as described in its prospectus.

Benefits of Mutual Funds

The benefits of owning mutual funds are unique and are very different from the benefits of owning individual stocks or bonds. These benefits range from offering immediate diversification to only requiring a small amount of money to purchase shares:

- **Diversification**—Mutual funds typically are comprised of a number of securities that cover a wide range of business sectors and industries. These areas could include: technology and communications; consumer, business, and financial services; consumer goods; industrial material; and energy and utilities. Such an array can help to spread risk and potentially reduce the impact of market fluctuations.

- **Asset allocation**—Most mutual funds focus on different categories and styles of investing. By combining several funds in your portfolio, you can develop a mixture of funds that could include stocks and bonds of large organizations, mid-size companies, small companies, and overseas companies, as well as funds that focus on a sector of the economy or a particular country. You get to decide the allocation. There are also styles of investing to consider. That is, there are mutual funds with a growth orientation or value orientation as well as funds that invest in a combination of growth and value—a blend orientation.

- **Professional management provided**—When you purchase shares in a mutual fund, you engage the services of a professional money manager or a team of money managers. They execute the day-to-day investment decisions that are consistent with the fund's objectives as articulated in the fund's prospectus.

- **Small transaction cost**—The cost is dependent on whether you purchase a "load" fund or a "no load" fund. Typically, with a Class A share load fund, there is an upfront sales charge of approximately 4.75 percent to 5.75 percent. With B and C shares, there is no upfront sales charge, but there is a deferred sales charge. With B shares, this deferred sales charge declines over several years and usually begins at around 5 percent to 6 percent. With C shares, there is typically a 1 percent deferred charge that lasts for one year. On the other hand, with "no load" funds there is no upfront or deferred sales charge.

- **Purchase amount relatively small**—Some funds allow initial purchases with as little as $250 with subsequent monthly investments as low as fifty dollars.

Summary

The initial phase in selecting mutual funds is determining the goal for your investment and your risk tolerance. These two factors should be kept in mind while selecting and evaluating mutual funds. When selecting mutual funds for review, the evaluation of each mutual fund's statistics against each other should be done in a manner consistent with each style and measure and factor. It's up to you to balance the result of the analysis between the qualitative measures and statistical factors and select those mutual funds consistent with your profile.

CHAPTER 4:
SELECTING MUTUAL FUNDS

Deciding which mutual funds to invest in is not simply a matter of some mystical force guiding your hand over a newspaper listing. Choosing is not easy; it's hard work.

To make the task manageable, use a process that is easy to understand and offers a logical sequence. The number of mutual funds you should analyze is based on:

1. the type of account you wish to have, for example, individual or regular account, IRA, or company-sponsored retirement account (usually a 401(k) or 403(b)); and,

2. the category and style of mutual funds that you want to select, such as a fund classified as large-cap value, small-cap growth, and so on.

Typically, your company-sponsored retirement plan will only have a few selections within any category and style of mutual fund. This differs from an IRA or regular account, for which the number of possible mutual funds can range from a few hundred to a few thousand. Qualitative measures and statistical factors should be used to provide the kind of information that allows you to progressively cull the available funds so that you end up with the most appropriate selections for you.

Whether it's an individual or regular account, an IRA, or a company-sponsored retirement account, following a process that guides your selection will provide the best results. The process I encourage you to follow is broken down into two major components: qualitative measures and statistical factors. While both major components are addressed, significant emphasis is placed on the statistical factors.

To obtain the actual data used in the process, I recommend you use the Morningstar™ Mutual Fund reports that can be found in the library or on www.morningstar.com.

To record the statistical information, you should use the worksheet that immediately precedes the Morningstar report on the following pages. When completed for all the mutual funds you wish to analyze in a certain category and style, the worksheet will hold the information you need to make your selection.

Several worksheets may be necessary. A separate worksheet should be completed for each category and style of mutual fund, such as large-cap value, mid-cap growth, and so forth. To illustrate this process, the Morningstar report for the Jensen Quality Growth J fund is used. This is a large-cap growth fund. The Morningstar report has been alphabetically notated (A–E) to quickly identify those measures and statistics that are discussed. (Morningstar reports are generally available at your local library.)

An abridged version of the process follows. The quality measures and statistical factors are described; however, the number of statistical factors has been limited to some of the more crucial. For a complete description of the mutual fund selection process, read Don's book, *Women & Mutual Funds: Gain Understanding and Be in Control.*

Qualitative Measures

Before you begin the statistical component of the process, you should pause and think about why you wish to invest. Your selection process should start by defining your goals or reasons for your investment. For example:

- Are you saving for retirement?
- Are you retired and seeking maximum income from your investment portfolio?
- Are you saving to make a significant purchase in the future?

Your goals or reasons for the investment will help you establish parameters. These include the amount of time you'll have before the money is needed. Also, you should decide on the level of risk you might be willing to accept to achieve the desired level of value to attain your goals. Your responses to the Risk Profile Questionnaire in chapter 6, on asset allocation, will help define your risk tolerance.

Another issue to examine is the kind of account you wish to establish. This will often dictate the time you'll need to develop a portfolio. For example:

- Is the investment a rollover from a 401(k) or 403(b)? In this instance, you may need the complete portfolio to be constructed.
- Is this an individual account that will focus on tax efficiency? This may require a totally new portfolio to be developed.
- Is it an IRA that will be used to complement your active 401(k) or 403(b)? A workplace retirement plan typically offers a limited number of categories and styles of funds from which to choose, so you may be in search of funds to close gaps in your workplace plan. Those gaps may include a large-cap value, a mid-cap growth, a small-cap value, or an international fund.

A third measure, Morningstar Pillars, provides an overall rating of a fund, which is the analysts' opinion about a fund's ability to outperform its peer group. Five pillars comprise the evaluation:

1. Process—indicates the quality of the selection process and the construction of the fund's portfolio
2. Performance—measures consistency of returns in different market conditions
3. People—evaluates the quality of the investment team
4. Parent—assesses the manner in which the fund is run and the degree to which the interests of management, the board of directors and investors are aligned
5. Price—the cost of the fund or its expense ratio

Refer to "A" in the Morningstar report. Jensen Quality Growth J fund has a gold rating, which on a scale of gold, silver, bronze, neutral, and negative is the highest rating.

Once you have completed the qualitative component of the process, you're ready to begin with the statistical factors. At this juncture, a note of caution is appropriate: Historical information is used to help you determine your portfolio, but it is important to know that a fund's past performance does not guarantee its future performance. That being said, history still remains an excellent guide to the future, when properly used.

Statistical Factors

We have tested many statistics to find the ones that proved to be the most beneficial in assisting us in the selection of mutual funds. This testing has resulted in the following statistical factors: percentile rank in category/mean (percent return); standard deviation, beta and R^2, and alpha. When these factors were used collectively, they provided the best guide for selecting mutual funds. These factors are explained below.

Percentile Rank in Category/Mean (Percent Return)

This is the first statistical factor we recommend for consideration. **Percentile rank in category/mean** is a measure that shows a mutual fund's rank, in terms of total return (percentile). It shows how a fund performed in relation to all the mutual funds in a particular category and style of investing. To view it from a different perspective, it would be the equivalent of a student's class ranking and grade point average within his or her academic major.

This factor is important because the fund's rank is the result of a myriad of variables that have influenced it over a period of time, for example, one, three, five, or ten years. The lower the number, the better the fund ranks in its class. So, for example, a rank of five is better than ten, and a rank of one is better than five. But what are some of the variables that could influence a fund's rank? These variables may include but are not limited to the portfolio manager's stock selection ability, the risks taken by the fund manager to achieve the returns, fund expenses, portfolio turnover, the state of the economy, earnings from the companies held in the fund, inflation, interest rates, and the political landscape. Time period is also an important consideration when trying to assess percentile rank in category. The best time frame is between five and ten years.

Refer to "B" in the Morningstar report. This factor is reported in four places. Jensen Quality Growth J fund was in the seventy-first percentile for all funds in this category and style and attained a return of 4.3 percent for one year. For the three-year, five-year, and ten-year periods, it ranked in the eighty-eighth, thirty-ninth, and thirty-eighth percentiles and returned 9.79 percent, 2.19 percent, and 3.92 percent, respectively. (Please note that the benchmark index is the Russell 1000 Growth Index.) The Statistical Analysis Worksheet that follows has been populated with these factors.

Statistical Analysis Worksheet

Mutual Fund Category <u>Large Cap</u>
Mutual Fund Style <u>Growth</u>

Qualitative Measure and Statistical Factors		Percent. Rank in Category/Mean			Measures of Risk			
Fund Name(s)	Rating	3 Years	5 Years	10 Years	Standard Deviation	Beta	R-Squared	Alpha
Jensen Quality Growth J	Gold	88 / 9.79%	39 / 2.19%	38 / 3.92%	17.83	0.88	93	-0.3

Data through October 31, 2011 Reprinted by permission of Morningstar.

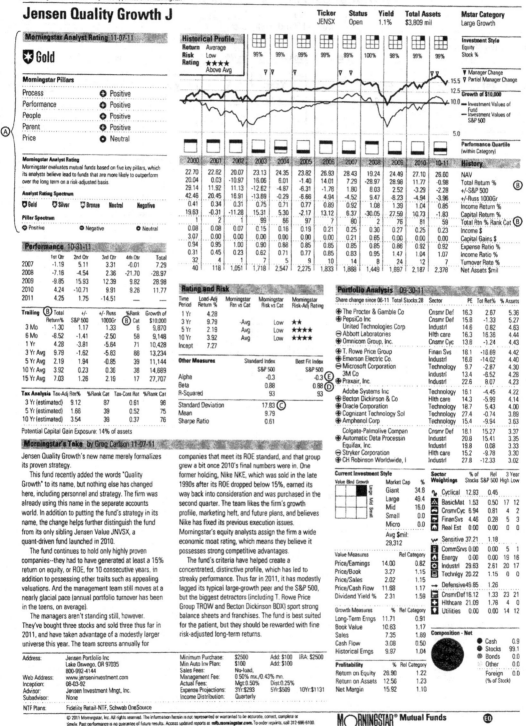

Jensen Quality Growth J

Ticker JENSX	**Status** Open	**Yield** 1.1%
Total Assets $3,809 mil	**Mstar Category** Large Growth	

Morningstar Analyst Rating 11-07-11

⭐ **Gold**

Morningstar Pillars

Process	➕	Positive
Performance	➕	Positive
People	➕	Positive
Parent	➕	Positive
Price	⬤	Neutral

Morningstar Analyst Rating

Morningstar evaluates mutual funds based on five key pillars, which its analysts believe lead to funds that are more likely to outperform over the long term on a risk-adjusted basis.

Analyst Rating Spectrum

🏅 Gold   🏅 Silver   🏅 Bronze   Neutral   Negative

Pillar Spectrum

➕ Positive   ⬤ Negative   ⬤ Neutral

Historical Profile

Return	Average
Risk	Low
Rating	★★★★ Above Avg

99% 99% 99% 99% 99% 100% 98% 99% 99%

Investment Style
Equity
Stock %

▼ Manager Change
▽ Partial Manager Change

Growth of $10,000
— Investment Values of Fund
— Investment Values of S&P 500

Performance Quartile (within Category)

	2000	2001	2002	2003	2004	2005	2006	2007	2008	2009	2010	10-11	History
	22.70	22.62	20.07	23.13	24.35	23.82	26.93	28.43	19.24	24.49	27.10	26.60	NAV
	20.04	0.03	-10.97	16.06	6.01	-1.40	14.01	7.29	-28.97	28.98	11.77	-0.98	Total Return %
	29.14	11.92	11.13	-12.62	-4.87	-6.31	-1.78	1.80	8.03	2.52	-3.29	-2.28	+/-S&P 500
	42.46	20.45	16.91	-13.89	-0.29	-6.66	4.94	-4.52	9.47	-8.23	-4.94	-3.96	+/-Russ 1000Gr
	0.41	0.34	0.31	0.75	0.71	0.77	0.89	0.92	1.06	1.39	1.04	0.85	Income Return %
	19.63	-0.31	-11.28	15.31	5.30	-2.17	13.12	6.37	-30.05	27.59	10.73	-1.83	Capital Return %
	1	2	1	99	66	97	7	80	2	76	81	59	Total Rtn % Rank Cat
	0.08	0.08	0.07	0.15	0.16	0.19	0.21	0.25	0.30	0.27	0.25	0.23	Income $
	3.07	0.00	0.00	0.00	0.00	0.00	0.00	0.21	0.65	0.00	0.00	0.00	Capital Gains $
	0.94	0.95	1.00	0.90	0.88	0.85	0.85	0.85	0.85	0.86	0.92	0.92	Expense Ratio %
	0.31	0.45	0.23	0.62	0.71	0.77	0.85	0.83	0.95	1.47	1.04	1.07	Income Ratio %
	32	4	1	7	5	9	10	14	8	24	12	7	Turnover Rate %
	40	118	1,051	1,718	2,547	2,275	1,833	1,888	1,449	1,697	2,187	2,378	Net Assets $mil

Performance 10-31-11

	1st Qtr	2nd Qtr	3rd Qtr	4th Qtr	Total
2007	-1.19	5.11	3.31	-0.01	7.29
2008	-7.16	-4.54	2.36	-21.70	-28.97
2009	-9.85	15.93	12.39	9.82	28.98
2010	4.24	-10.71	9.91	9.26	11.77
2011	4.25	1.75	-14.51	—	—

Trailing	Total Return%	+/- S&P 500	+/- Russ 1000Gr	%Rank Cat	Growth of $10,000
3 Mo	-1.30	1.17	1.33	6	9,870
6 Mo	-8.52	-1.41	-2.50	58	9,148
1 Yr	4.28	-3.81	-5.64	71	10,428
3 Yr Avg	9.79	-1.62	-5.83	88	13,234
5 Yr Avg	2.19	1.94	-0.85	39	11,144
10 Yr Avg	3.92	0.23	0.36	38	14,689
15 Yr Avg	7.03	1.26	2.19	17	27,707

Tax Analysis	Tax-Adj Rtn%	%Rank Cat	Tax-Cost Rat	%Rank Cat
3 Yr (estimated)	9.12	87	0.61	96
5 Yr (estimated)	1.66	39	0.52	75
10 Yr (estimated)	3.54	39	0.37	76

Potential Capital Gain Exposure: 14% of assets

Rating and Risk

Time Period	Load-Adj Return %	Morningstar Rtn vs Cat	Morningstar Risk vs Cat	Morningstar Risk-Adj Rating
1 Yr	4.28			
3 Yr	9.79	-Avg	Low	★★
5 Yr	2.19	Avg	Low	★★★★
10 Yr	3.92	Avg	Low	★★★★
Incept	7.27			

Other Measures	Standard Index S&P 500	Best Fit Index S&P 500
Alpha	-0.3	-0.3
Beta	0.88	0.88
R-Squared	93	93
Standard Deviation	17.83	
Mean	9.79	
Sharpe Ratio	0.61	

Morningstar's Take by Greg Carlson 11-07-11

Jensen Quality Growth's new name merely formalizes its proven strategy.

This fund recently added the words "Quality Growth" to its name, but nothing else has changed here, including personnel and strategy. The firm was already using this name in the separate accounts world. In addition to putting the fund's strategy in its name, the change helps further distinguish the fund from its only sibling Jensen Value JNVSX, a quant-driven fund launched in 2010.

The fund continues to hold only highly proven companies--they had to have generated at least a 15% return on equity, or ROE, for 10 consecutive years, in addition to possessing other traits such as appealing valuations. And the management team still moves at a nearly glacial pace (annual portfolio turnover has been in the teens, on average).

The managers aren't standing still, however. They've bought three stocks and sold three thus far in 2011, and have taken advantage of a modestly larger universe this year. The team screens annually for

companies that meet its ROE standard, and that group grew a bit once 2010's final numbers were in. One former holding, Nike NKE, which was sold in the late 1990s after its ROE dropped below 15%, earned its way back into consideration and was purchased in the second quarter. The team likes the firm's growth profile, marketing heft, and future plans, and believes Nike has fixed its previous execution issues. Morningstar's equity analysts assign the firm a wide economic moat rating, which means they believe it possesses strong competitive advantages.

The fund's criteria have helped create a concentrated, distinctive profile, which has led to streaky performance. Thus far in 2011, it has modestly lagged its typical large-growth peer and the S&P 500, but the biggest detractors (including T. Rowe Price Group TROW and Becton Dickinson BDX) sport strong balance sheets and franchises. The fund is best suited for the patient, but they should be rewarded with fine risk-adjusted long-term returns.

Address:	Jensen Portfolio Inc Lake Oswego, OR 97035 800-992-4144	Minimum Purchase:	$2500	Add: $100	IRA: $2500
		Min Auto Inv Plan:	$100	Add: $100	
		Sales Fees:	No-load,		
Web Address:	www.jenseninvestment.com	Management Fee:	0.50% mx./0.43% mn.		
Inception:	08-03-92	Actual Fees:	Mgt:0.50%	Dist:0.25%	
Advisor:	Jensen Investment Mngt. Inc.	Expense Projections:	3Yr:$293	5Yr:$509	10Yr:$1131
Subadvisor:	None	Income Distribution:	Quarterly		
NTF Plans:	Fidelity Retail-NTF, Schwab OneSource				

Portfolio Analysis 09-30-11

Share change since 06-11 Total Stocks:28

	Sector	PE	Tot Ret%	% Assets
⊕ The Procter & Gamble Co	Cnsmr Def	16.3	2.67	5.36
⊕ PepsiCo Inc	Cnsmr Def	15.8	-1.33	5.27
⊖ United Technologies Corp	Industrl	14.6	0.82	4.63
⊖ Abbott Laboratories	Hlth care	16.3	16.36	4.44
⊕ Omnicom Group, Inc.	Cnsmr Cyc	13.8	-1.24	4.43
⊕ T. Rowe Price Group	Finan Svs	16.6	-16.69	4.42
⊕ Emerson Electric Co.	Industrl	16.6	-14.02	4.40
⊖ Microsoft Corporation	Technology	9.7	-2.87	4.30
3M Co	Industrl	13.4	-6.52	4.28
⊕ Praxair, Inc.	Industrl	22.6	8.07	4.23
Adobe Systems Inc	Technology	16.1	-4.45	4.22
⊕ Becton Dickinson & Co	Hlth care	14.3	-5.99	4.14
⊕ Oracle Corporation	Technology	18.7	5.43	4.00
⊕ Cognizant Technology Sol	Technology	27.4	-0.74	3.89
⊕ Amphenol Corp	Technology	15.4	-9.94	3.63
Colgate-Palmolive Compan	Cnsmr Def	18.1	15.27	3.37
⊕ Automatic Data Processin	Industrl	20.8	15.41	3.35
Equifax, Inc.	Industrl	19.8	0.08	3.33
⊖ Stryker Corporation	Hlth care	15.2	-9.78	3.30
⊖ CH Robinson Worldwide, I	Industrl	27.8	-12.33	3.02

Current Investment Style

Value Blnd Growth — Large Mid Small

Market Cap	%
Giant	34.6
Large	49.4
Mid	16.0
Small	0.0
Micro	0.0
Avg $mil:	29,312

Value Measures		Rel Category
Price/Earnings	14.00	0.82
Price/Book	3.27	1.05
Price/Sales	2.03	1.15
Price/Cash Flow	11.68	1.17
Dividend Yield %	2.31	1.59

Growth Measures	%	Rel Category
Long-Term Erngs	11.71	0.91
Book Value	10.63	1.17
Sales	7.35	1.89
Cash Flow	3.08	0.50
Historical Erngs	9.97	1.04

Profitability	%	Rel Category
Return on Equity	26.90	1.22
Return on Assets	12.56	1.23
Net Margin	15.92	1.10

Sector Weightings	% of Stocks	Rel S&P 500	3 Year High Low	
⤴ Cyclical	12.93	0.45		
🏭 BasicMat	1.53	0.50	17	12
🏢 CnsmrCyc	6.94	0.81	4	2
💰 FinanSvs	4.46	0.28	5	3
🏠 Real Est	0.00	0.00	0	0
⤳ Sensitive	37.21	1.18		
📡 CommSrvs	0.00	0.00	5	1
⚡ Energy	0.00	0.00	19	16
⚙ Industrl	29.63	2.61	20	17
💻 Technlgy	20.22	1.15	0	0
→ Defensive	49.85	1.26		
🛒 CnsmrDef	16.12	1.33	23	21
➕ Hlthcare	21.09	1.76	4	0
🔌 Utilities	0.00	0.00	14	12

Composition - Net

	%
⬤ Cash	0.9
⬤ Stocks	99.1
⬤ Bonds	0.0
⬤ Other	0.0
Foreign (% of Stock)	0.0

MORNINGSTAR® Mutual Funds

Standard Deviation, Beta, and R²

These statistics are generally accepted as the most often-used indices to measure risk. Risk in its simplest form is defined as the possibility of loss.

Standard deviation measures the difference between the actual returns of a fund (over time) and the average return for that fund over the same time period. It shows how far the actual returns deviate from the average return. The importance of standard deviation is that it accepts as a given the many factors that influence a fund's return. The larger the standard deviation, the farther away from the average a typical return lies. The farther away an actual return lies from the average return, the greater the risk associated with that mutual fund. This is evidenced by a high standard deviation number.

Refer to "C" in the Morningstar report. Jensen Quality Growth J fund has a standard deviation of 17.83 percent. (This calculation is based on data over the past thirty-six months.) This means that 68 percent of the returns of the fund fell between plus or minus 17.83 percent of its average return. Using the three-year average return of 9.79 percent, this range of returns is between +27.63 percent to -8.03 percent. This range is arrived at in the following manner:

Upper Range: Take the average return of 9.79 percent and add the standard deviation of +17.83 percent. This yields an upper range of +27.63 percent. (Remember that standard deviation is both a positive and negative number.)

Lower Range: Take the average return of 9.79 percent and subtract the standard deviation of -17.83 percent. This yields a lower range of -8.03 percent.

Another way to explain standard deviation is by comparing the grade point average of two students, Amy and Martha. Let's say Amy's average was higher than Martha's. The conclusion that could be easily reached is that Amy was a better overall student than Martha. But by investigating the details, we learn that Amy's average was made up of more As and Cs but fewer Bs than Martha's. From the details, we can conclude that while Amy's average was higher, her individual grades were more spread out than Martha's. So, while Amy's grade point average was higher, she experienced greater risk in attaining that average (receiving more of the lower grade of C and thus requiring more As). Would you be comfortable taking on the added risk to possibly achieve a higher return?

Beta, on the other hand, measures the degree of variation or volatility of a fund's return in relation to a benchmark or market index given the numerous influences in the marketplace. This benchmark index can be the S&P 500, for example. The benchmark index always has a value of 1.00. This measure (beta) is important because it isolates the amount of risk in a fund as it is compared to the benchmark index. In using this factor, utilize the "best fit" beta as the benchmark beta because it better reflects the underlying characteristics of the portfolio.

What does this mean? Beta is another measure of volatility and shows the degree of risk a fund possesses. Unlike standard deviation that shows the volatility inherent in a fund, beta compares the riskiness of a fund to that fund's benchmark index. However, a low beta doesn't necessarily mean that a fund has a low degree of volatility.[15] It means that the fund's market-related risk is low.[16] So how do you know how much risk is market-related? This is supported by the r-squared (r^2) statistic, or the coefficient of determination. What is r^2?

R^2 shows how much of a fund's return can be explained by the fund's "best fit" benchmark index.[17] The higher the r^2 of the fund, the higher the certainty that the fund's volatility is attributable to this benchmark index. The higher the r^2, the more relevant the beta is to the fund's return. Other factors that can cause volatility that are outside beta include industry risk and company risk.

Refer to "D" in the Morningstar report. Jensen Quality Growth J fund has a beta of 0.88 when measured against its benchmark index and an r^2 of 0.93. (This calculation is based on data over the past thirty-six months.) What does this mean? It means that nearly all of the fund's beta or volatility is explained by the benchmark index. If, let's say, the index gained 10 percent, the fund's return should theoretically rise 9.3 percent (which is 93 percent of the total increase). Conversely, if this index showed a 10 percent decline, the fund should theoretically drop 9.3 percent (again, by 93 percent of the decrease). Here, too, the higher the number, the greater the fund's volatility.

These concepts—standard deviation, beta, and r^2—are central to the mutual fund selection process. Once you've become comfortable with these measures of risk and come to understand and accept the extent of variation or the amount of volatility you're able to cope with, your attention can then be turned to a fund's alpha statistic.

---

15 *Morningstar Principia Mutual Funds.* CD-ROM. March 2006.
16 Ibid.
17 Ibid.

Alpha

Alpha shows the ability of a fund to generate returns that are higher or lower than the fund's expected return given the fund's level of risk. The risk measure that underscores the determination of alpha is the fund's beta. The alpha is expressed as a percentage. The higher the positive number, the better; the higher the negative number, the worse. This is explained below.

The importance of alpha is that it represents a level of return generated by a mutual fund that is above or below the level the fund's beta would have predicted. To put it another way, alpha is a measure that shows how well the portfolio manager has done the job of managing the fund and adding incremental value beyond the fund's return expectations.

When referring to "E" in the Morningstar report, Jensen Quality Growth J fund's alpha was -0.3 percent when computed using the S&P 500 index. (This calculation is based on data over the past thirty-six months.) This negative statistic means that the fund achieved a result lower than the market's expectation, or, to say it another way, the Jensen Quality Growth J fund slightly underperformed the market. If the fund achieved the market's expectation, its alpha would have been equal to zero. If it outperformed the market's expectation, the number would have been positive.

Alpha can be found in many facets of daily life and certainly outside of the investment arena. For example, let's say you decide to take a two-week vacation. You put together a detailed itinerary that, when priced out, costs $10,000. This includes airfare, hotels, meals, entertainment, and other expenses. However, before making the arrangements, you visit a travel agent and ask the agent to price it out. The travel agent comes back with a price tag of $9,000. The alpha in this instance would be $1,000—the extra value the travel agent could bring to your vacation plans.

Summary

The initial phase in selecting mutual funds for your portfolio is determining the goal for the investment and your risk tolerance. These two factors should be kept in mind while selecting and evaluating the mutual funds. These factors become even more important in understanding asset allocation. When selecting mutual funds for review, recording the key factors of those mutual funds is crucial. Mutual funds should be analyzed by category and style. For example, all large-cap value funds should be on the same technical analysis worksheet.

For emphasis, the key factors are summarized below:

1. Percentile rank in category/mean (percent return)
2. Standard deviation, beta, and r^2
3. Alpha

Once you've recorded the information on the statistical analysis worksheets, the evaluation of each mutual fund's statistics against each other is done in a manner consistent with the definition and explanations of each measure. Now you must make certain decisions. It's up to you to balance the qualitative measures and the statistical factors and select those mutual funds that are most consistent with your profile.

CHAPTER 5:
OTHER INVESTMENTS USED FOR RETIREMENT

When it comes to investing for retirement, either in an IRA, 401(k), 403(b), etc., mutual funds are typically the most commonly used investment vehicle. However, investments used for retirement funding should not be restricted to mutual funds. There are other investment choices available.

The purpose of this chapter is to discuss these other investment choices and provide information that will allow you to determine whether one or more of these alternatives are suitable for you. (The authors wish to thank Wikipedia, the free online encyclopedia, for providing the definitions of the other investment choices.) We have selected the more common investment choices; however, we do not discuss certificates of deposit (CDs). Also, we avoid introducing arcane and little-understood investments, such as collateralized mortgage obligations (CMOs), put and call options, etc.

Of the investment choices introduced, we have summarized some of their important features. However, a more detailed list of features is provided for each investment choice in the table at the end of the chapter.

Exchange-Traded Funds (ETF)

An exchange-traded fund, like a mutual fund, holds a basket of assets and is valued based on the value of each holding. However, a mutual fund is only valued and traded once a day—after the close of the market. On the other hand, an exchange-traded fund trades throughout the trading day. This ability to trade the funds throughout the trading day provides ongoing liquidity. The upside potential for growth and potential downside risk is similar to a mutual fund's growth and risk.

The type of tax levied on any income or capital gain earned is dependent on whether the ETF is held in a tax-deferred retirement account or in a taxable account. If the ETF is held in a tax-deferred retirement account, any income distributed from the account is subject to ordinary income tax. If, however, the ETF is held in a taxable account, any dividend, capital gain, or interest distributed from the account is subject to their respective tax rates.

When compared to a mutual fund, exchange-traded funds offer the following:

Advantages:
1. Trades throughout the trading day
2. Trades at market price, which may be higher (seller's advantage) or lower (buyer's advantage) than net asset value
3. Offers upside growth potential
4. Offers diversification

Disadvantages:
1. Price can be volatile
2. Return of investment principal is not guaranteed

Closed-End Funds

A closed-end fund has certain characteristics of a mutual fund and of an exchange-traded fund. Like a mutual fund, a closed-end fund contains a basket of diversified securities. These funds may be actively managed or traded, though some are not. Similar to an ETF, a closed-end fund can be bought and sold throughout the trading day, providing ongoing liquidity. The risk associated with owning a closed-end fund is similar to that of an exchange-traded fund and a mutual fund.

The taxable nature of any income or capital gains earned is predicated on the type of investment vehicle in which the closed-end fund is held. If held inside an IRA or other tax-deferred retirement vehicle, distributions will be taxed as ordinary income. If there is a cost basis in the IRA from nondeductible contributions, any gain can be reduced by this cost basis on your federal income tax return. When held in a taxable account, not an IRA or qualified retirement plan, dividends are taxed at the appropriate dividend rate, capital gains or losses are taxed at the capital gains rate, and any interest income is taxed at the ordinary tax rate.

When compared to a mutual fund, closed-end funds offer the following:

Advantages:
1. Trades throughout the trading day
2. Trades at market price, which may be higher (seller's advantage) or lower (buyer's advantage) than net asset value
3. Offers upside growth potential
4. Offers diversification

Disadvantages:
1. Price can be volatile
2. Can sell at a premium to net asset value
3. Return of investment principal is not guaranteed

Common Stocks

Common stock denotes ownership in a company. Ownership of common stock conveys certain rights that other investment alternatives don't have. These rights include but are not limited to voting on company policies, electing the board of directors, stock splits, new offerings of stock, and in some instances, determining senior management compensation. The riskiness of common stock can be described by how an owner would fare in case of bankruptcy. In the event of bankruptcy, common stock holders receive funds after creditors, bondholders, preferred stockholders, etc. When compared to a mutual fund, typically the upside potential of a common stock is greater than that of a mutual fund; however, the downside risk of loss is greater than that of a mutual fund. The biggest advantages of the mutual fund are that it provides diversification among many different stocks and is managed by a professional.

If a common stock is held within a tax-deferred retirement account, dividends and capital gains, when distributed, are subject to ordinary income tax. Common stock doesn't issue interest payments. Conversely, if the stock is held inside a taxable account, dividends are subject to the appropriate dividend tax rate and capital gains are subject to the appropriate capital gains tax rate.

When compared to a mutual fund, common stock offers the following:
Advantages:
1. Trades throughout the trading day
2. Trades at market price, which may be higher (seller's advantage) or lower (buyer's advantage) than net asset value
3. Offers upside growth potential

Disadvantages:
1. Price can be volatile
2. Offers no diversification
3. Return of investment principal is not guaranteed

Preferred Stocks

Preferred stock is a special kind of equity that has some features of a common stock as well as some characteristics of a debt instrument. In case of a company's liquidation, preferred stocks are senior to common stock but subordinate to bonds. "Senior" means that preferred stockholders are paid before common stockholders. An important similarity between preferred stocks and common stock is that dividends may be offered; a key similarity between preferred stock and debt (bonds) is that both are rated by the major credit agencies.

The taxability of dividends and capital gains on preferred stock is the same as common stock. The factor that determines the type of tax that is applied is the type of account in which the preferred stock is held—tax-deferred retirement account or taxable account.

When compared to a mutual fund, preferred stock offers the following:
Advantages:
1. Trades throughout the trading day
2. Trades at market price, which may be higher (seller's advantage) or lower (buyer's advantage) than net asset value
3. Return of investment principal at par is guaranteed when called or at maturity
4. Provides dividend income

Disadvantages:
1. Limited upside growth potential
2. Price can be volatile
3. Offers no diversification

Treasury Securities

Treasury securities are government debt issued by the United States Department of the Treasury. We will confine our discussion to the four types of marketable Treasury securities: Treasury bonds, Treasury notes, Treasury bills, and Treasury Inflation Protected Securities (TIPS).

- **Treasury bond:** A Treasury bond is a debt instrument that has the longest maturity of Treasury issues—from twenty to thirty years. It has a coupon payment every six months; the secondary market (where these issues can be sold before maturity) is very liquid. At maturity, the owner receives the face value of the bond.

- **Treasury note:** A Treasury note is a debt security that matures in one to ten years. It has a coupon payment every six months like the Treasury bond. Similar to the Treasury bond market, the Treasury note market is highly liquid. At maturity, the owner receives the face value of the note.

- **Treasury bill:** A Treasury bill has a maturity of one year or less. It does not pay interest prior to maturity, but it is sold at a discount from the face value of the Treasury bill. At maturity, the owner receives the face value of the bill.

- **Treasury Inflation-Protected Securities:** TIPS are inflation-indexed bonds issued by the Treasury. They are offered with five-, ten-, and thirty-year maturities. The principal amount is adjusted by the Consumer Price Index. Even though the coupon rate doesn't change, TIPS generate a different amount of interest when multiplied by the inflation-adjusted principal.

If a Treasury security is held in a taxable account, interest income, while subject to federal income tax, is exempt from state tax. Any capital gain is subject to federal and state tax. On the other hand, if the Treasury security is held in a tax-deferred retirement account, taxes on interest income and capital gains are postponed until that money is withdrawn. At that time, any interest income or capital gains is subject to ordinary federal income tax.

When compared to a mutual fund, Treasury securities offer the following:

Advantages:
1. Trades throughout the trading day
2. Trades at market price, which may be higher (seller's advantage) or lower (buyer's advantage) than coupon
3. Risk-free—guaranteed by the US government
4. Redeemed at maturity at par value
5. Interest income not taxable by state and local government, when outside an IRA or qualified plan

Disadvantages:
1. Limited upside growth potential
2. Interest rates may be lower than other fixed income investments
3. Offers no diversification

Municipal Bonds

A municipal bond (MUNI) is a type of security that is issued by a state, city, or local government, including their agencies. MUNIs may be general obligations of the issuer or secured by specific revenues.

If the MUNI is held in a taxable account, income is generally federal- and state-tax free. Any capital gain, though, is subject to federal and state tax. If the MUNI is held in a tax-deferred retirement account, taxes on interest income and capital gains are postponed until the money is withdrawn. At that time, any interest income or capital gain is subject to ordinary income tax.

When compared to a mutual fund, municipal bonds offer the following:

Advantages:
1. Trades throughout the trading day
2. Trades at market price, which may be higher (seller's advantage) or lower (buyer's advantage) than coupon
3. Redeemed at maturity at par value
4. Interest income is fully tax-free when held outside of a qualified plan or IRA
5. Interest payments are guaranteed by issuing municipality

Disadvantages:
1. Limited upside growth potential
2. Depending on the rating of the bond, liquidity may be an issue
3. Interest rates may be lower than other fixed income investments
4. Offers no diversification

Corporate Bonds

A corporate bond is a debt instrument (essentially an IOU) that is issued to raise money for expansion or some other company purpose. Typically, the maturity of these bonds can be for five or more years. Corporate bonds are often listed on major exchanges as well as traded in the over-the-counter markets. Generally, corporate debt is categorized as secured vs. unsecured and senior vs. subordinate.

- **Secured Debt:** This form of IOU is a loan in which the borrower pledges assets as collateral. In the event that the borrower defaults, the creditor takes possession of the assets.
- **Unsecured Debt:** This refers to any type of debt obligation that is not backed by any kind of collateral. If there is a default, the unsecured creditor will have a claim on the general assets after the secured creditors have been satisfied.
- **Senior Debt:** This is debt that takes priority over subordinate or "junior" debt of the issuer if the issuer goes bankrupt.
- **Subordinated Debt:** This is debt that is "junior" or subordinate to senior debt.

If the corporate bond is held in a taxable account, interest income is subject to federal and state income tax. Similarly, any capital gain is subject to federal and state tax. On the other hand, if the corporate bond is held in a tax-deferred retirement account, taxes on interest income and capital gains are postponed until the money is withdrawn. At that time, any interest income or capital gains are subject to ordinary Federal income tax.

When compared to a mutual fund, corporate bonds offer the following:
Advantages:
1. Trades throughout the trading day

2. Trades at market price, which may be higher (seller's advantage) or lower (buyer's advantage) than coupon
3. Redeemed at maturity at par
4. Interest rates are typically higher than other fixed income investments
5. Interest payments are guaranteed by issuing company

Disadvantages:
1. Upside growth potential may be limited
2. Depending on the rating of the bond, liquidity may be an issue
3. Oftentimes these bonds are issued without explicit guarantees or collateral

Unit Investment Trusts (UIT)

A unit investment trust (UIT) is a fixed, unmanaged portfolio of stocks or bonds that has a definite life. There are essentially two types of trusts: stock trusts and bond trusts.

A stock trust is designed for capital appreciation and/or dividend income. A specific number of units is sold with an established termination date. At the date of termination, the trust liquidates and distributes the net asset value to the holders of the unit trust.

A bond trust, like a stock trust, has a predetermined termination date. A bond trust pays monthly income, usually a consistent amount, until the first bond in the trust is called or matured. From this point until the trust terminates, a lesser amount of consistent income is paid monthly. A bond trust is most appropriate for individuals who seek current income and principal stability.

If the trust is held in a taxable account, dividends, interest income, and capital gains are subject to federal and state income tax. However, if the trust is held in a tax-deferred retirement account, taxes on dividends, interest income, and capital gains are postponed until the money is withdrawn. At that time, any and all income is subject to ordinary federal income tax.

When compared to a mutual fund, UITs offer the following:
Advantages:
1. Offers diversification
2. May offer tax-free income
3. May have access to investment opportunities not otherwise available

Disadvantages:

1. Is not traded throughout the trading day, but is priced at the end of the trading day
2. Trades at market price, which may be higher (seller's advantage) or lower (buyer's advantage) than coupon
3. Upside growth potential is limited
4. Does not offer income guarantees
5. Investment principal is not guaranteed

Annuities

According to the US Securities and Exchange Commission, an annuity is a contract with an insurance company. This contract calls for the purchaser to either make a lump-sum investment or periodic investment payments. In return, the insurance company agrees to either make a lump-sum distribution or periodic payments for a specified period of time, including for life. There are four basic types of annuities: immediate, fixed, variable, and equity-indexed.

- **Immediate Annuity:** It is purchased with a single payment made to an insurance company. This payment is immediately converted into a stream of periodic income payments. These payments are guaranteed for the insured's lifetime.

- **Fixed Annuity:** This type of annuity can be purchased with either a single payment or multiple payments made to an insurance company. In return, the insurance company guarantees that you will earn a minimum rate of interest while your account grows. Furthermore, the insurance company guarantees that, when the time comes, you can select a periodic payment schedule that can last for your lifetime or the lifetime of you and your spouse.

- **Variable Annuity:** Like the fixed annuity, a variable annuity is one where the purchaser can either make a single payment or multiple payments to the contract during the growth or accumulation phase. The difference is with a variable annuity, the investment options are selected from a series of mutual funds. The level of periodic payments received from the insurance company is based on the performance of those mutual funds. Performance is not guaranteed.

- **Equity-Indexed Annuity:** Like the fixed and variable annuity, the equity-indexed annuity can be purchased with a single payment or multiple payments. The performance of this annuity is based on the performance of a selected index (i.e., S&P 500). Usually the insurance company will guarantee a minimum return (oftentimes, it's zero); in return for that no-loss guarantee, the insurance company will place a limit on the upside potential gain. For example, the insurance company may offer a guarantee that your account will not lose money; however, it could place a limit on your potential maximum by limiting such gain to 60 percent of the index's gain.

An annuity is always a tax-deferred account. During the accumulation (or pre-distribution phase), no taxes are paid. Any distribution received by you is subject to ordinary income tax. However, usually a portion of any distribution is a return of principal and not subject to tax. As with other investments, if held inside an IRA or other tax-deferred retirement vehicle, distributions will be taxed as ordinary income. The tax rules are complex, and you should consult with a qualified tax professional.

When compared to a mutual fund, annuities offer the following:
Advantages:
1. May offer diversification
2. Insurer provides income guarantees
3. Insurer provides investment principal guarantees

Disadvantages:
1. Is not traded throughout the trading day
2. With the exception of immediate annuity, usually not liquid.
3. Income payments are usually fixed for life—no cost-of-living adjustments
4. Once annuitized, annuitant forfeits ownership of principal
5. Management fees may be higher

Rental Real Estate

When held outside a retirement account, property purchased for the express purpose of renting can provide a steady stream of cash flow. This gross cash flow is subject to ordinary federal and state income tax—after all related expenses are deducted. Rental real estate can also be held in an IRA or other retirement account. The tax rules are complex, and you should consult with a qualified tax professional.

When compared to a mutual fund, rental real estate offers the following:

Advantages:
1. Provides a monthly cash flow
2. Offers upside growth potential
3. Costs of upkeep and maintenance are tax-deductible

Disadvantages:
1. Generally not liquid
2. No diversification is offered
3. Subject to market risk—potential deterioration of value

Investment Real Estate

When held outside a retirement account, property purchased for the express purpose of selling it upon retirement can provide a lump sum for retirement planning needs. The gain or loss generated from the transaction is subject to ordinary income tax—after all related expenses are reported on federal and state income tax returns. Investment real estate can be held in an IRA or other retirement account. The tax rules are complex, and you should consult with a qualified tax professional.

When compared to a mutual fund, investment real estate offers the following:

Advantages:
1. Offers upside growth potential
2. Mortgage interest and real estate tax are deductible
3. Capital improvements can be added to the cost basis of the property

Disadvantages:
1. Generally not liquid

2. Offers no diversification
3. Subject to market risk—potential deterioration of value

Life Insurance

Life insurance is a contract between a policy owner and an insurance company. The insurance company agrees to pay a designated beneficiary a sum of money based upon an event—usually the death of the insured. Life insurance contracts fall into two major categories: investment policies and protection policies.

Investment policies are designed to facilitate the growth of capital by regular premiums or a single premium. Additionally, it builds cash value. The most common forms are variable life, universal life, and whole life.

- **Variable Life Insurance:** This form of insurance is like the variable annuity. While the premium is fixed, the amount of insurance and cash value varies based on the performance of the underlying investments. The investments that are available come from the insurance company's portfolio of stocks, bonds, equity mutual funds, and bond funds. Even though the variable life insurance policy has the greatest upside potential for cash value growth, it also has the greatest downside risk. As such, the premium is the most expensive of the three investment-type policies. Generally, the cash value can be used to pay some if not all of the annual premium. And the annual dividends paid by the policy can be withdrawn by the policyholder without terminating the policy.

- **Universal Life Insurance:** This type of insurance offers a combination of low-cost insurance, like term insurance, and a savings portion that represents any excess premium paid. Over time, this excess premium builds as cash value. This cash value can be used to offset the annual premium or withdrawn to supplement retirement income.

- **Whole Life Insurance:** This form of cash value life insurance is the most conservative. It calls for a level premium for the lifetime of the insured. Any amount of premium paid in excess of the cost of insurance is conservatively invested. A portion of the excess premium goes to build cash value. Any remaining portion of excess dividends can be used to offset the annual premium or withdrawn to supplement retirement income.

Protection policies provide a benefit based upon the occurrence of an event, usually the policyholder's death. The most common form of protection policy is term life.

- **Term Life Insurance:** This life insurance option provides protection based on an insurance rate that is fixed over a specific time frame. Once the specified time frame expires, the policy can be renewed at a higher rate for a new specified period of time. The premium paid is equivalent to the cost of insurance; there is no cash value buildup. Since there is no cash value buildup, this should not be used when formulating a retirement strategy. Furthermore, this form of insurance is not generally used for estate-planning purposes.

Life insurance policies are given favorable tax treatment. The cash surrender value is not taxed to the policy owner. Death benefits, whether investment or protection, are not presently taxed to the beneficiaries. If, however, an investment policy is terminated, any excess cash value (over the policyholder's investment) is taxed at the termination of the contract.

Investment-type life insurance can be an effective retirement planning strategy. It cannot be purchased as an IRA investment, but can be an investment inside a qualified retirement plan. A common strategy referred to as Private Pension is pre-funding an investment policy to build cash values. The Private Pension is using nonqualified money—money that is not in an IRA or qualified retirement plan. This strategy allows the owner to accelerate the insurance payments to build the cash value more quickly, which then allows the account owner to borrow from the policy. Insurance policy loans generally do not require repayment, but taking loans may decrease the value of the death benefit. Purchasing life insurance as a retirement planning strategy should be carefully considered and discussed with your financial advisor and tax professional.

Insurance offers the following:
Advantages:
1. Provides financial protection in the event of an untimely death
2. Tax-deferred growth and tax-free death benefit to beneficiaries upon death of the owner
3. Provides liquidity to the estate of the deceased

4. Cash value policies can provide income during lifetime of the owner through policy loans

Disadvantages:
1. Generally not liquid
2. Management fees are higher
3. Cannot be an investment in an IRA

Long-Term Care Insurance

As with life insurance, long-term care insurance (LTC) is a contract between a policy owner and an insurance company. The insurance company agrees to pay a designated beneficiary a sum of money based upon an event—in this case, the inability to perform activities of daily living. LTC helps defray the cost of care either in the home by a family member, in a skilled nursing facility, or in an assisted living facility.

LTC is considered an important component when planning for retirement income security. It provides protection so that your retirement assets won't be used to pay for assisted care. LTC is typically purchased between the ages of forty-five and sixty-five. It can be purchased at later ages; however, the cost will be significantly higher, and an older purchaser runs the risk of poorer health. Some employers offer long-term care insurance as part of their employee benefit package.

Long-term care insurance offers the following:

Advantages:
1. Distributions are tax-free
2. Provides protection in the event of incapacity or need for assistance with daily living activities
3. Premiums are generally tax deductible
4. Offsets the out-of-pocket cost of assisted living

Disadvantages:
1. Generally not liquid
2. Management fees are high
3. Cannot be an investment in an IRA
4. Benefit may not be needed because client maintains health

Summary

The following table captures features and reflects the typical use of the different investment choices described in this chapter. Please refer to specific descriptions within the chapter for more detail. An "X" indicates generally no; a checkmark indicates generally yes; "N/A" indicates doesn't apply. With the exception of the last feature, items represented in the table reflect nonqualified investments, meaning not held as an investment within an IRA or other type of retirement plan.

Features/Investment Choices	Mutual Funds	Closed End Fund	Fund/Exchange Traded	Common Stock	Preferred Stock	Treasury Securities	Municipal Bonds	Corporate Bonds	UIT	Annuities	Rental Real Estate	Estate/Investment Real	Life Insurance	LTC
Traded throughout day	X	√	√	√	√	√	√	√	X	X	X	X	X	X
Liquidity: can be sold quickly	√	√	√	√	√	√	√	√	√	√	X	X	X	
Tax free income	Varies by type	Varies by type	Varies by type	X	X	√	√	X	√	X	X	X	X	√
Management fees	√	√	√	X	X	X	X	X	X	√	√	√	√	√
Transaction/ticket charges	X	√	√	√	√	√	√	√	X	X	√	√	X	X
Growth potential	√	√	√	√ X	X	X	X	X	Varies by type	√	√	√	X	X
Guaranteed return of principal: get par value back	X	X	X	X	√	√	√	√	X	√	X	X	X	X
Insured/guaranteed	X	X	X	X	X	√	√	X	X	√	X	X	√	√
Income Guarantees	X	X	X	X	X	√	√	√	X	√	X	X	X	√
Provides income	Varies by type	Varies by type	Varies by type	Varies by type	√	√	√	√	√	√	√	X	X	√
Price volatility	√	√	√	√	√	√	√	√	√	√	√	√	X	X
Premium/discount to NAV or face value	X	√	√	N/A	√ X	√ X	√ X	√ X	X	X	X	X	X	X
Leverage	√	√	Varies by type	√	√	X	X	X	X	X	X	√	X	X
Diversified: mixture of holdings	√	√	√	X	X	X	X	X	√	√	X	X	X	X
More volatility, hence more risk than mutual fund	X	X	X	√	√	X	X	X	X	X	√	√	X	X
Vote on company matters	√	√	√	√	X	X	X	√	X	X	N/A	N/A	X	X
IRA or Qualified plan investment	√	√	√	√	√	√	√	√	√	√	√	√	X	X

Summary

CHAPTER 6:
ASSET ALLOCATION

Simply put, asset allocation is the balancing of an investment portfolio among stock mutual funds, bond mutual funds, and cash. (Be aware that asset allocation does not ensure a profit and does not protect against losses in a declining market.) This chapter on asset allocation will give you a basic understanding of and inform you of the importance of allocating your investment dollars among different categories and styles of mutual funds.

To begin to understand asset allocation, we must answer two questions at the outset:
1. Why is it important to balance or allocate your investment portfolio?
2. What has academic research offered that demonstrates the degree, if any, that mutual fund portfolio returns are affected by asset allocation?

Let's begin with an example of asset allocation in action.

A Comparative Example of the Asset Allocation Process

Asset allocation, in many ways, is like planning a wedding. The real value is in the details. In asset allocation, you delineate your investments into two styles—value and growth. (While blend funds represent a third style, it is excluded from this discussion. Blend funds are a combination of value and growth.) You then refine each style by segmenting them into categories that may include domestic equity funds, international equity funds, bonds, and cash. The categories and styles can be further defined by the size of the fund's holdings—large cap, mid-cap, and small cap.

From this point, you determine the amount of your total investment that should go into each component in your attempt to attain an optimal portfolio or result. To return to our comparative example, in planning a wedding, there are two significant areas of concern—the ceremony and the reception. From here, you break down each area into those components that could affect the outcome of the wedding. You then attempt to determine the impact each component could have on the wedding and apportion to each component the necessary time, attention, and money to achieve an optimal result—a flawless wedding.

Importance of Asset Allocation

Asset allocation functions as a risk control mechanism. Using asset allocation, the investor—you—seeks to reduce the effects of market volatility by attempting to balance risk among a portfolio's investments. (Generally, the risk of loss associated with stocks or stock mutual funds is greater than that of bonds or bond mutual funds. And the risk of loss associated with bonds or bond mutual funds is greater than that of cash.) Asset allocation is one of the primary means for attempting to manage risk at a level that is comfortable for you. Asset allocation attempts to address three significant areas of investor concern:

1. Investment goals and objectives
2. Tolerance for risk
3. Time requirements before the funds are needed

As an investor, once you've figured out where you stand on the above-listed concerns, you can proceed to allocate your assets based on:

1. The best combination of stock mutual funds and bond mutual funds
2. The most appropriate blend of domestic mutual funds and international mutual funds
3. The most suitable mix of stock mutual funds among large cap, mid-cap, and small cap, as well as value and growth funds

Quantitative Impact of Asset Allocation

The conclusion reached in a 1986 watershed study[18] and confirmed in a 1991 follow-up study[19] was that asset allocation was responsible for a significant portion of the variation in quarterly portfolio returns. Since the 1991 study, there have been several other papers[20] that have validated the conclusions reached in 1986 and 1991. However, the

---

18 Brinson, Gary P., Randolph Hood, and Gilbert L. Beebower. "Determinants of Portfolio Performance." *Financial Analysts Journal,* July/August 1986.

This seminal study on asset allocation involved the analysis of ninety-one large pension funds from 1974 to 1983. The study concluded that, on average, 93.6 percent of the quarterly variation in plan results was attributed to asset allocation. Furthermore, the study concluded that less than 5 percent in the quarterly variation of plan results was caused by security selection.

19 Brinson, Gary P., Brian D. Singer, and Gilbert L. Beebower. "Determinants of Portfolio Performance II: An Update." *Financial Analysts Journal,* May/June 1991.

In this study, the impact of passive and active asset allocation and security selection was analyzed. This analysis studied eighty-two large pension plans that covered the period 1977–87. It concluded that passive asset allocation explained 91.5 percent of the variation in quarter-to-quarter portfolio returns.

This is demonstrated in the Callan Periodic Table of Investment Returns. This table shows the returns achieved by each category, large-, mid-, and small-capitalization companies, and style, value, and growth of investment. For the current twenty-year period, 1987–2006, in only one instance did one category and style lead the pack for more than two consecutive years. From 1995 through 1998, large company stocks achieved returns of 38.1 percent, 24 percent, 36.5 percent, and 42.2 percent, respectively. Predicting the category and style of investment that will lead the pack by year's end is much like trying to pick the winning lottery number. A few may be fortunate, but many will be utterly disappointed.

20 Jahnke, William. "The Asset Allocation Hoax." *Journal of Financial Planning,* February 1997.

This analysis revisited the Brinson, Hood, and Beebower study of 1986 and found it to be flawed. According to the author, the 1986 study focused on portfolio volatility and not on portfolio returns. Because of this, the average percentage cited—93.6 percent—pertained to the variation in quarterly results and not the variation in the rate of returns. The conclusion reached by the author was that asset allocation explained only 14.6 percent of the total return (not the 93.6 percent noted in the 1986 study).

Singer, Brian. "Hoax and Strawmen." *Journal of Financial Planning,* October 1997.

Evensky, Harold. "The Hoax Is a Hoax." *Financial Planning,* November 1997.

Wilson, Philip. "Mad as Hell." *Dow Jones Investment Advisor,* February 1998.

Beebower, Gilbert, Michael Hogan, and Robert Ludwig. "Asset Allocation: Is It a Hoax?" *SEI,* Spring 1998.

Statman, Meir. "The Numbers Racket Rages On." *Financial Planning,* April 1998.

Ibbotson, Roger G., and Paul D. Kaplan. "Does Asset Allocation Policy Explain 40, 90, or 100 Percent of Performance?" Available at www.ibbotson.com/research, December 1998, revised April 1999.

"Asset Allocation: Revisiting the Debate." *Morningstar,* February 27, 1997.

degree or magnitude of the impact remains in question and will probably be debated for years. (You don't have to go any farther than the recession of 2009 to see the effect of asset allocation or a lack of asset allocation. If you were fully invested and concentrated in stocks or equity mutual funds during this time, you probably lost a significant portion of your portfolio's value.)

Other Reasons for Asset Allocation

An underlying rationale for asset allocation is that the investment category or style that ends up at year-end to be the market leader is not easily predictable. Through the use of asset allocation, however, you're able to participate in the overall success of the market and at the same time, possibly reduce your risk of loss. This is because all types of investments don't move in the same direction or to the same extent or have the same risk characteristics.

Advantages and Disadvantages of Asset Allocation

There are essentially two fundamental advantages that asset allocation offers:[21]

1. A means to attempt to optimize the return on your investment portfolio. You seek to achieve portfolio returns according to the level of risk you believe you can tolerate.
2. A way to create and control risk by avoiding the proverbial "putting all your eggs into one basket."

The one major disadvantage of asset allocation is the possibility of missing opportunities.[22] For example, during the period 1995 to 1998, if your investment portfolio was concentrated in large-cap holdings, your average yearly return would have exceeded 35 percent. In all likelihood, this level of return exceeded that of any portfolio allocated among large-cap, mid-cap , small-cap, and international holdings. However, to have anticipated such a recurrence, particularly for four consecutive years, was highly remote, if not impossible.

---

21 Darst, David M. *The Art of Asset Allocation.* New York: McGraw-Hill Companies, 2003.
22 Ibid.

Risk Profile Questionnaire

Three factors are the primary drivers in the determination of asset allocation. These factors are your investment goals and objectives, your risk tolerance, and your expectation of the time needed to achieve the intended result.

Before you consider the risk and time factors, it is important that you clearly define your goals and objectives for the portfolio. For example, your goals could include but certainly are not limited to:

1. Retirement
2. Supplemental income
3. Education of children or grandchildren
4. Special purchase, such as a vacation home or an extended vacation

In trying to come to terms with your tolerance for risk, we recommend that you use a questionnaire that delves into basic feelings about taking risks. An example of such a questionnaire appears at the end of this chapter. When answering the questions, your responses should be consistent with and be reflective of your intended goals for the portfolio. They should incorporate your feelings and thoughts when it comes to the possible loss of a portion of your portfolio's value. And, of course, your replies should be made with due consideration given to the amount of time the portfolio will have to grow. (Typically, the longer the time horizon to achieve your goals, the more tolerant of risk you may be.)

The Risk Profile Questionnaire[23] comprises nine questions. The first eight questions are in standard format. That is, each question presents an issue and offers possible replies. You select the response that is most suitable and comfortable for you. The last question, however, is in tabular form. It shows four hypothetical portfolios and the returns they achieve over a five-year period. Even though a five-year period is shown, the four portfolio options should be examined together one year at a time. To do this, cover up the years that remain to be examined. Then gauge your reaction to each hypothetical portfolio's performance and select the portfolio best suited for you before you proceed to the next year. This should be done for each of the five years. There are no correct answers. The purpose of this questionnaire is to show tendencies and to find a consistent pattern to your responses.

---

23   Gudhus, Donald S. *Women & Mutual Funds: Gain Understanding and Be in Control.* Bloomington, IN: iUniverse, 2008.

RISK PROFILE QUESTIONNAIRE

_____		_____
Name		Date

There are no right or wrong answers. Simply check the answer that is most representative.
The following answers are not to be construed as investment instructions in the event that the scenarios depicted actually occur.

1. How long do you think you will retain this investment portfolio?

   - [ ] 0   3 to 5 years
   - [ ] 1   5 to 10 years
   - [ ] 2   over 10 years

2. Is it important for you to receive money from your account on a monthly basis?

   - [ ] 1   Yes, it is very important and it must be the same amount each month.
   - [ ] 2   It is important, but growth of my portfolio is also an important factor.
   - [ ] 3   It is not important, because growth of my portfolio is my primary goal.

3. Your feelings about investing can best be summed up as:

   - [ ] 1   I would accept a moderate long-term rate of return rather than worry about my account losing money.
   - [ ] 2   I can accept fluctuations in my account value if it means a higher potential return over the long run.
   - [ ] 3   I want the maximum opportunity for long-term growth in my account and I am willing to accept significant year-to-year fluctuations in the value of my account.

4. Six months after you make a $100,000 investment it decreases in value by $25,000 in a down market period. Not knowing what the future will bring, how would you feel?

   - [ ] 1   Very uncomfortable. I would consider selling my investment.
   - [ ] 2   Uncomfortable, yet I would stay with the investment if my financial advisor recommended it.
   - [ ] 3   I would want to buy more of the investment, since this is a good investment opportunity.

5. Although past performance is no guarantee of future results, stocks or stock mutual funds have historically provided better protection against inflation than bonds or bond mutual funds. And through diversification, a portfolio of stocks or stock mutual funds also provides the potential for less volatility in returns. But historically, stock or stock mutual funds have been more volatile than bond or bond mutual funds. How do you feel about stocks or stock mutual funds?

   - [ ] 1   I don't want them in my portfolio.
   - [ ] 2   I would use them in my portfolio.
   - [ ] 3   I think stock or stock mutual funds are very attractive and should occupy a dominant position in my portfolio.

6. While small companies tend to have higher expected returns, they typically add more risk to your portfolio. How do you feel about having small companies in your portfolio?

   - [ ] 1   I don't want to add more risk to my portfolio.
   - [ ] 2   If my advisor recommends it, I would agree to it.
   - [ ] 3   Should be used to appropriately allocate my portfolio. And, I am aware of the increased risk.

RISK PROFILE QUESTIONNAIRE

Name	Date

7. A well diversified portfolio generally includes overseas investments. However, that could add more risk to your portfolio, particularly in the short-term. How do you feel about having overseas holdings in your portfolio?

	1	I don't want to add more risk to my portfolio.
	2	If my advisor recommends it, I would agree to it.
	3	Should be used to appropriately allocate my portfolio. And, I am aware of the increased risk.

8 In addition to considering small company and international mutual funds, consideration should be given to including commodity and emerging market mutual funds. Understand that such mutual funds can add more risk and volatility to your portfolio. How do you feel about including these holdings in your portfolio?

	1	I don't want to add more risk to my portfolio.
	2	If my advisor recommends it, I would agree to it.
	3	Should be used to appropriately allocate my portfolio. And, I am aware of the increased risk.

9 Below is a table showing five years of hypothetical returns for four hypothetical portfolios, A to D. A to D get progressively riskier. With which hypothetical portfolio do you feel most comfortable? (**Please note:** The rates of return shown below are purely hypothetical and do not represent the performance of any individual investment or portfolio of investments. They are for illustrative purposes only and should not be used to predict future product performance. Specific rates of return, especially for extended time periods, will vary. There is also a higher degree of risk associated with investments that offer the potential for higher rates of return.)

Instruction:
LOOK AT EACH SELECTION FOR THE 5-YEAR PERIOD. LOOK AT EACH YEAR CONSECUTIVELY. HOW DO YOU FEEL AFTER EACH YEAR? WITH WHICH TREND ARE YOU THE MOST COMFORTABLE AND TOLERANT, GIVEN THE FACT THAT YOU'RE NOT SUPPOSED TO KNOW WHAT THE FOLLOWING YEAR OR YEARS WILL BRING?

		Invest Now	Year 1	Year 2	Year 3	Year 4	Year 5	Average
A	0	$100,000	$103,000 (+3%)	$106,100 (+3%)	$109,300 (+3%)	$112,600 (+3%)	$115,900 (+3%)	3.0%
B	1	$100,000	$106,000 (+6%)	$106,000 (0%)	$96,500 (-9%)	$110,000 (+14%)	$117,700 (+7%)	3.6%
C	2	$100,000	$110,000 (+10%)	$103,400 (-6%)	$83,800 (-19%)	$108,900 (+30%)	$120,900 (+11%)	5.2%
D	3	$100,000	$111,000 (+11%)	$93,200 (-16%)	$74,600 (-20%)	$108,100 (+45%)	$122,200 (+15%)	7.0%

"Risk Profile Questionnaire Score." See below. Compare that number to those arranged and classified in the "Investor Profile." See below.

RISK PROFILE QUESTIONNAIRE SCORE _____

INVESTOR PROFILE

	Risk Profile Score			Risk Profile Score
Conservative Income	7 - 10	Growth		19 - 22
Income	11 - 14	Maximum Growth		23 - 26
Conservative Growth	15 - 18			

After a detailed examination of your answers (combined with your selected mutual funds), the next step is to create a diversified portfolio that meets your needs and goals. That's easier said than done. But we'll do it!

Try to find the kind of portfolio that gives you the maximum expected return for the least amount of risk assumed (as measured by standard deviation)—the optimal return. The stock mutual fund portion of your portfolio generally includes more categories and styles of investment than the bond mutual fund portion. Because of this complexity, I find it easier in the development of an investment portfolio to begin with the fixed component. Based on the risk profile score achieved from the questionnaire, the following table presents a guideline on the relative size of the fixed component or bond mutual fund portion that should be considered for your investment portfolio.

Risk Profile Score	Suggested Percent of Bonds
Maximum Growth: 23–26	3%–0%
Growth: 19–22	15%–6%
Conservative Growth: 15–18	44%–21%
Income: 11–14	58.00%
Conservative Income: 7–10	75.00%

Summary

In many ways, asset allocation is like various things we do in everyday life. The example of planning a wedding has many similarities to asset allocation because it involves appropriately apportioning a finite amount of money to each of several activities. The end result, of course, is to have a special wedding.

Whether it's planning a wedding, devising a family's budget, or creating an investment portfolio, asset allocation is important because it can be used to construct an optimal result: the highest achievable gain given a certain level of risk. In asset allocation, you're spreading your investment over a variety of opportunities, as opposed to concentrating it in only one or two opportunities. So even though maximizing your return may not be possible, you should be able to reduce your downside risk exposure.

An effective way of determining the level of risk you can tolerate is by completing the Risk Profile Questionnaire. This survey seeks replies to questions that, when analyzed, can be translated into your risk profile score. This risk profile score functions as a starting point in creating your asset allocation.

However, when it comes to quantifying the benefit that asset allocation offers, it becomes a little tenuous, as the various referenced studies indicate. But while the exact benefit remains elusive, these academic studies undoubtedly show that there is a quantifiable benefit.

CHAPTER 7:
RETIREMENT PLAN DISTRIBUTIONS AND TAX IMPLICATIONS

Now that you have gained a basic appreciation and awareness of the various types of retirement plans available, the nuances that are an integral part of each of the plans, the maximum annual contributions allowed, and a way to save for retirement through the use of mutual funds and other investment choices, let's turn our attention to getting your money out of your retirement plan—and any tax implications (with regard to any state tax implications, we recommend consulting your tax advisor).

General Distribution Rules

IRAs

Traditional IRA
The account owner can withdraw money at any time from an IRA account. Distributions are federally taxed as ordinary income in the year of the withdrawal, with the exception of cost basis. Cost basis in an IRA is after-tax money rolled from an employer plan or contributions you made to the IRA that were not deductible. Be aware that if money is taken from the IRA prior to attaining age 59 ½, you, the IRA owner, will be subject to an early withdrawal penalty of 10 percent on the full amount withdrawn, unless there is an exception.

The exceptions to the early withdrawal penalty are referred to as 72(t) exceptions, corresponding to the Internal Revenue Code that governs these early withdrawals. The most common exceptions to the 10 percent penalty are:

1. Age 59 ½, as previously mentioned
2. Death
3. Disability
4. The receipt of substantial and equal periodic payments

Additional early withdrawal exceptions may apply to your specific situation. Consult a financial advisor or tax professional for assistance when taking distributions if you are under age 59 ½.

Let's use an example to see how the most common exceptions to the 10 percent penalty apply to our hypothetical investor, Julie. The first exception is attaining age 59 ½. Once Julie has attained age 59 ½, she may withdraw money without the worry of the 10 percent early withdrawal penalty. She must be past age 59 ½ before taking a distribution to avoid the 10 percent early withdrawal penalty. Be careful, and seek advice from your financial advisor.

If Julie passes away at age 45, Julie's beneficiary will be able to take distributions from Julie's IRA without penalty, regardless of age. However, Julie's beneficiary will be required to pay tax on the distribution because withdrawals are taxed in the year withdrawn. We'll discuss tax implications to the beneficiary in chapter 8.

If, instead of passing away, Julie became disabled, she may be able to withdraw her IRA balance without incurring the early withdrawal penalty. Julie must meet the definition of disability in order to avoid the early withdrawal penalty. One of the criteria is that the disability will result in death or be of indefinite duration. As a general rule, if Julie qualifies for Social Security disability, she should be able to take distributions from her retirement account without an early withdrawal penalty. She would still, however, pay federal income tax on the distribution, and some states may also tax the withdrawal. This is something you should discuss with your financial advisor or tax professional.

The fourth way mentioned above to avoid the 10 percent early distribution penalty and obtain income is through substantial and equal periodic payments. These payments require a precise formula for taking the distributions. One of three methods must be used to determine the distribution amount:

1. Life expectancy payments

2. Amortization
3. Annuitization

Once the payments start, the payments must continue for five years or until the account owner turns age 59 ½, whichever date is later.

Let's look at a hypothetical: Susan starts substantial and equal periodic payments from her IRA the year she turns 53. She must continue the payments until she attains age 59 ½ to avoid being penalized on all of her distributions taken to date. Her friend Marc, who started his distributions the year he turned age 57, would need to continue the payments until after the completion of the five-year period, which will be during the year Marc turns age 62. Again, payments must be for a minimum of five years from the date payments started.

As mentioned above, the distributions must follow a precise formula to meet the exception. Let's look at the different methods of calculation:

1. The life expectancy method is calculated by taking the December 31 prior year–ending IRA account balance and dividing it by your current-year life expectancy. This calculation is done each year, and the amount will vary yearly as the account owner gets older and as the year-end account balances change. This method provides the lowest annual distribution.

2. Amortization and annuitization are similar in that both factor in growth in the accounts. Under the amortization method, the annual payment is determined by the following factors: the value of the account, the individual's life expectancy, and interest rate. Under the annuitization method, the annual payment is determined by dividing an individual's account balance by an annuity factor. The annuity factor is a table of numbers calculated by actuaries, which is provided by the IRS for this calculation. The calculation uses life expectancy, an interest factor that is stipulated monthly by the IRS, and, usually, the prior year–ending account balance. This amount, once identified, does not change from year to year.

Your financial advisor or tax professional can assist you with this calculation. There are online calculators that can make this calculation, also. Two are dinkytown.com and 72t.net. Please be aware that there are steep penalties if the calculation is changed within the required time frame. The early withdrawal penalty can be assessed back to the first distribution. So, once this distribution is started, don't stop or add money to the account until you have consulted with your financial advisor.

In 2002, the IRS recognized that clients were locked into payment schedules that no longer were reasonable and could result in significant depletion of their IRA accounts. The IRS issued a notice that allowed a one-time change to the calculation. This allowed the IRA owner to change from the amortization or annuitization method to the life expectancy method, thereby lowering the payments. You might take advantage of this one-time election if you no longer need the money, for example, if you were laid off and then went back to work. Be careful with this one as well. Once elected, you won't be able to change your mind.

Distributions from the traditional IRA must begin after the individual has attained age 70 ½. We'll discuss Required Minimum Distributions later in this chapter.

Roth IRA

Like the traditional IRA, the Roth IRA allows the account owner to take distributions at any time. There are two types of money in the Roth IRA: contributions and earnings. If the Roth IRA is held for five years and meets one of the following four provisions, the contributions and earnings will be tax-free when distributed. The four provisions are:

1. Death
2. Disability
3. Age 59 ½ or older
4. First-time home purchase

Since contributions are made with after-tax money, the contributions can be withdrawn at any time without penalty. The earnings may be subject to income tax and early withdrawal penalties if the earnings are taken prior to meeting one of the above requirements. Let's look at how the Roth distribution rules impact taxation and penalties using an example.

Jamie contributed $2,000 every year for the past ten years to her Roth IRA. Her Roth IRA is currently worth $23,000. Because she has been investing in the account for the past ten years, she has met the five-year holding period. Now, if Jamie is 46, she can take out $20,000 from the Roth IRA without paying income tax. If she also withdrew the $3,000 of earnings, that amount would not only be subject to ordinary income tax, it would also be subject to a penalty unless she was using the Roth IRA money to purchase her first home or if she meets the definition of being disabled.

Samantha also has contributed to her Roth IRA for ten years. She is 62 years old and wants to withdraw money. Since she is over age 59 ½ and has had the account for more than five years, Samantha can take distributions up to the entire value of her Roth IRA without paying federal income tax or an early withdrawal penalty.

Ginger converted a traditional IRA to a Roth IRA and would like to take money from the Roth IRA. Generally, a conversion requires the federal income tax to be paid in the year of conversion, thereby changing the tax status of the IRA from pre-tax to after-tax money. The conversion requires the converted amount to be held in the Roth IRA for five years to avoid the early withdrawal penalty of 10 percent, discussed earlier under traditional IRAs. The same penalty exceptions apply as noted above for Roth IRAs.

Unlike the traditional IRA, distributions from a Roth IRA are not required to begin after the individual has attained age 70 ½. We'll discuss Required Minimum Distributions later in this chapter.

Beneficiary IRA

This type of IRA allows distributions at any time. Because the beneficiary IRA could be a traditional or a Roth IRA, the taxation will depend on the type of account. The beneficial owner will not incur the early withdrawal penalty, regardless of his or her age, since the distribution is due to the death of the original account owner. When the account owner passes away, the custodian will require the account title be changed to include the beneficiary in the account title. An example would be John Beneficiary of Dorothy Smith IRA.

Whether the account is a beneficial traditional IRA or a beneficial Roth IRA, distributions by the beneficiary are required and must begin the year following the death of the account owner. Distributions will be taxable based on whether the account is a traditional IRA or a Roth IRA. See previous sections on how traditional IRAs, deductible or nondeductible, and Roth IRAs, are taxed. We'll discuss Required Minimum Distributions due to death of the IRA owner in chapter 8.

Spousal IRA

The spousal IRA can also be categorized as either a traditional IRA or a Roth IRA and follows the rules outlined above. Money can be withdrawn at any time, but distributions may be subject to federal income taxes and possibly state income tax, as well as the early withdrawal penalty.

Distributions must begin after the individual has attained age 70 ½ only if the account is a traditional IRA. However, with the death of the account owner, distributions must begin the year following the year of the account owner's death for either a traditional IRA or Roth IRA. We'll discuss Required Minimum Distributions later in this chapter.

Payroll Deducted IRA

This, too, can be categorized as either a traditional IRA or Roth IRA and follows the rules outlined above. Money can be withdrawn at any time, but will be subject to income taxes and if withdrawn before attaining age 59 ½, may be subject to the 10 percent early withdrawal penalty.

Distributions must begin after the individual has attained age 70 ½ if the account is a traditional IRA. However, with the death of the account owner, distributions are required the year following the year of the account owner's death if the account is a traditional IRA or Roth IRA. We'll discuss Required Minimum Distributions later in this chapter.

Rollover IRA

This type of IRA follows the same rules as a traditional IRA or Roth IRA, depending on the account type. Rollover IRAs indicate that the original source of the money was an employer-sponsored retirement plan, either funded by the employee or the employer.

Withdrawals can be made at any time but may be subject to early withdrawal penalties. A rollover Roth IRA will come from a 401(k) that allowed designated Roth salary deferrals.

Distributions must begin after the individual has attained age 70 ½ if the account is a traditional IRA, or the year following the year of the account owner's death if the account is a traditional IRA or Roth IRA. We'll discuss Required Minimum Distributions later in this chapter.

Employer-Funded Retirement Plans

Simplified Employee Pension Plan (SEP IRA)

SEP IRAs follow IRA rules. However, a SEP contribution is only made by the employer and contains only pre-tax money. After-tax contributions cannot be made to a SEP IRA. When distributions are made from the SEP IRA, the distributions are taxable as ordinary income and may be subject to early withdrawal penalties, unless one of the 72(t) exceptions previously discussed apply to the distribution. The SEP IRA assets can be removed at any time by the account owner. There are no restrictions on taking money out of the SEP IRA, but as mentioned earlier, the distributions will be taxed and may be subject to the early withdrawal penalties. Distributions from the SEP, like the IRA, must begin once the account owner has attained age 70 ½. These distributions will be described later, in the section on Required Minimum Distributions.

Profit-Sharing Plan

Like the SEP IRA, a profit-sharing plan is generally funded by the employer with pre-tax money. Distributions of pre-tax contributions from a profit-sharing plan are taxable as ordinary income and may be subject to early withdrawal penalties. The profit-sharing plan might contain after-tax contributions where federal income tax has already been paid. After-tax contributions, even if withdrawn prior to attaining age 59 ½, are not subject to tax or the 10 percent early withdrawal penalty when distributed. However, any earnings are subject to tax as ordinary income. Check with the plan administrator to determine if after-tax money is present in the plan.

In contrast to the SEP IRA, the profit-sharing plan restricts the ability of the employee to distribute money from the plan until a specified event occurs. The specific events are outlined in the plan document and may include:

1. Death
2. Disability
3. Reaching early retirement age as specified in the plan
4. Reaching normal retirement age
5. Separation from service
6. Plan loans
7. In-service distributions, which may include financial hardship
8. Separation from service after attaining age 55 (not age 59 ½ as with IRAs)

The plan administrator can help you determine if you qualify for a loan or an in-service distribution. Plan loans are not taxable when acquired, but may become taxable if payments aren't made on time, you quit, or you are laid off. In-service distributions are distributions made while you are still employed. One type of in-service distribution is caused by hardship that can be taken to avoid substantial financial hardship. Distributions made after separation from service and after attaining age 55 do not incur an early withdrawal penalty.

Distributions must be taken after the account holder has attained age 70 ½ or after that individual has separated from service, whichever is later. If you are still working after age 70 ½, you may be able to delay taking distributions until you have separated from service, providing it is allowed in the plan. This ability to delay RMDs does not apply to 5 percent or more business owners and their immediate family members.

Money Purchase Pension Plan

As mentioned in chapter 1, these plans are not as prevalent as they once were. The money purchase pension plan contains only employer contributions and generally will have distribution provisions and income tax consequences similar to those described under the profit-sharing plan.

Stock Bonus Plan

Since the stock bonus plan is a type of profit-sharing plan or money purchase pension plan, it follows the distribution and tax rules outlined above for profit-sharing plans.

Target Benefit Plan

The target benefit plan is similar to the money purchase pension plan and follows those distribution rules, tax rules, and restrictions.

Defined Benefit Plan

The defined benefit plan is funded by the employer with pre-tax money. These plans restrict the ability of the employee to distribute money from the plan until a specified event occurs. The specific events are outlined in the plan document and include death and disability. Some plans do not allow distributions upon reaching early retirement age or separation from service. Check with the plan administrator regarding plan specifics.

Unlike the profit-sharing plan, defined benefit plans generally will not allow hardship or in-service distributions; however, it may allow loans. Finally, any distribution taken before age 59 ½ will be penalty-free if the distribution is taken during the year attained age 55 (not age 59 ½) or later and due to separation from service.

An exception to the age-55 rule applies to distributions made to police, fire, and other public safety employees. Penalty-free distributions are allowed to be made after attaining age 50 and after separation from service. The plan administrator can assist you with specific plan terms that might restrict your ability to make withdrawals. Distributions, however, must begin after you have reached age 70 ½ or separated from service, whichever is later. If you are still working after age 70 ½, you may be able to delay taking distributions until you have separated from service, if the plan allows. This ability to delay RMDs does not apply to 5 percent or more business owners and their immediate family members.

Distributions are considered ordinary income and subject to taxation and early withdrawal penalties.

Cash Balance Plan

Since the cash balance plan is a type of defined benefit plan, it follows the defined benefit plan distribution requirements.

Fully Insured Defined Benefit Plans: 412(e) Plan

This type of defined benefit plan is invested in life insurance and annuities and follows the defined benefit plan distribution rules. Federal taxation of distributions is consistent with rules governing the defined benefit plan. However, careful consideration must be made prior to taking distributions from these plans, since large distributions could cause the underlying insurance policy to lapse.

There are two sets of rules that must be followed:
1. Retirement plan distribution rules that restrict distributions
2. The insurance policy distribution restrictions

If the insurance policy doesn't maintain its funding requirements, the policy will lapse and become worthless. Any distributions from a 412(e) plan should be discussed with your plan administrator prior to requesting distributions.

Life insurance in a qualified retirement plan has a special provision that allows the individual to purchase the insurance policy from the plan after the life insurance has been in the plan for at least two years. One important consideration with insurance in the retirement plan is that the insurance cannot be rolled over to an IRA when distributed from the retirement plan.

Employee-Funded Retirement Plans (Salary Deferral Plans)

SIMPLE IRA
SIMPLE IRAs follow the IRA distribution rules outlined previously. To recap:
- Can be withdrawn at any time.
- Taxed as ordinary income when distributed.
- No after-tax or Roth contributions can be made to a SIMPLE IRA.
- Must start distributions at age 70 ½: no exceptions.
- Distributions prior to age 59 ½ may be subject to the early withdrawal penalty (see 72(t) exceptions).

SARSEP
SARSEPs also follow IRA distribution and tax rules. As mentioned earlier, these plans can no longer be opened. Also, they generally do not have after-tax contributions, and Roth contributions cannot be made. Distributions must start when the individual attains age 70 ½, there are no exceptions, and distributions prior to the individual attaining 59 ½ may be subject to the early withdrawal penalty.

Traditional 401(k) and Safe Harbor 401(k) Plans
Like the profit-sharing plan, either type of 401(k) restricts the owner's ability to withdraw money from the plan prior to separation from service. There are, however, three exceptions:
1. Death
2. Disability
3. Attaining normal retirement age

The plans typically allow loans and in-service distributions. Any distributions taken after separation from service and after attaining age 55 are not subject to an early withdrawal penalty. Note that this is different from traditional IRAs, which do not allow penalty-free distributions prior to age 59 ½.

Distributions must be taken after the individual has attained age 70 ½ or after the individual has separated from service, whichever is later. If you are still working after age 70 ½, you may be able to delay taking distributions until you have separated from service, if the plan allows. This ability to delay RMDs does not apply to 5 percent or more business owners and their immediate family members. Distributions are considered ordinary income and subject to federal income tax.

403(b) or Tax-Sheltered Annuity (TSA) Plans

Typically, this plan allows distributions to begin upon attaining age 59 ½. They follow the profit-sharing plan rules and often restrict distributions to the following reasons:

1. Death
2. Disability
3. Separation from service

Any distributions taken after separation from service and after attaining age 55 can be taken without incurring the early withdrawal penalty. Note that this is different from traditional IRAs, which do not allow penalty-free distributions prior to age 59 ½.

Distributions must be taken after the individual has attained age 70 ½ or after the individual has separated from service, whichever is later. If you are still working after age 70 ½, you may be able to delay taking distributions until you have separated from service if the plan allows. Federal taxation of distributions follows the rules of the 401(k).

457(b) Plan

These plans are available to city, county, other governmental entities, and non-profit organizations. They follow the same rules as the 403(b) plan. Individuals can take distributions from the plan after separation from service and after attaining age 55 without incurring the 10 percent early withdrawal penalty.

Distributions must be taken after the individual has attained age 70 ½ or after the individual has separated from service, whichever is later. If you are still working after age 70 ½, you may be able to delay taking distributions until you have separated from service if the plan allows. Distributions are considered ordinary income and subject to federal income tax.

Other Types of Retirement Plans

Employer Stock Ownership Plan (ESOP)

These plans are diverse and it is best to speak with the plan administrator regarding distribution options. Generally, distributions may be made in-kind, in the form of shares of company stock. Special tax treatment is afforded qualified plans that distribute employer stock in-kind. Distributions usually are taxed as long-term capital gains when the stock is distributed. There is a strategy called "NUA" treatment. "NUA" stands for Net Unrealized Appreciation. This special tax treatment allows an individual to delay paying taxes on any NUA portion of the in-kind stock distribution. Taxation is delayed until the employer's stock is sold. This strategy should be discussed with your tax professional.

Nonqualified Deferred Compensation Plan

There is specific language in the plan documents for nonqualified deferred compensation plans as to when distributions must be taken, when distributions are taxable, and in some cases, when "phantom income" is triggered. Phantom income occurs when an individual is taxed as if she has taken a distribution from the plan, even though a distribution from the plan was not made. Most plan distributions are taxed as additional payroll and show up on your W-2. Since these distributions are not eligible to be rolled to an IRA, they are not subject to the early withdrawal penalties and are not subject to the Required Minimum Distribution (RMD) rules when the individual turns 70 ½.

Required Minimum Distributions (RMD)

Money cannot remain in an IRA or retirement plan indefinitely. As described under each specific plan type, owners of traditional IRA-based plans must start distributions when age 70 ½ is reached; there are no exceptions. Roth IRAs do not require minimum distributions while the account owner is alive. Upon the account owner's death, distributions must begin. The required distribution rules are different depending on the type of retirement plan. These rules are referred to as Required Minimum Distributions.

IRAs

Traditional IRA

Distributions from a traditional IRA are required to start by April 1 of the year following the year the account holder turns 70 ½. Subsequent distributions must be taken each year by December 31.

Let's look at Mary. Her 70th birthday was May 14, 2012. Mary turned 70 ½ on November 14, which is six months after her 70th birthday. By law, she was required to take a distribution from her traditional IRA by April 1, 2013, that is, April 1 of the year following the year Mary turned 70 ½. If, instead of May 14, 2012, Mary's birthday was August 4, 2012, she would have turned 70 ½ in February 2013. In this case, her first distribution would be required by April 1, 2014.

The IRS grants an additional three months for the first RMD. So, if Mary took her first distribution by April 1, 2013, she in fact would take two distributions in 2013—one for the year she turned 70 ½ (in 2012) and the other, her normal 2013 distribution. Mary could have taken her RMD by December 31 of the year she turned 70 ½ (in 2012) to avoid taking two RMDs in the same year. Mary should discuss her situation with her financial advisor or tax professional when she turns 70 ½ to identify the best strategy for her.

The RMD is calculated by taking the previous December 31 ending account balance and dividing it by the account holder's current-year life expectancy. IRS Life Expectancy Tables can be found in IRS Publication 590, which is available on the website www.irs.gov. Your financial advisor or tax professional can assist with the calculation.

Required Minimum Distributions that are not taken on time incur a 50 percent penalty on any amount that was not taken and that should have been taken. IRA custodians must provide an annual notice reminding the IRA account owner that an RMD is required for the year. In most cases, the IRA custodian will provide the calculation based on the account balance. However, the IRA custodian is not responsible for making the calculation on all IRA accounts held by the account owner, since not all the accounts may be held with that IRA custodian.

If you have multiple IRA accounts, you should make the RMD calculation for each of the accounts. The IRS allows you to take the RMD amount from any or all IRA accounts. It's your decision. For example, Mary has two IRA accounts and is required to withdraw $5,000 this year. She can take the entire $5,000 from one of the accounts or split the distribution between the two accounts.

These calculations can become difficult when working with IRAs invested in annuities because the current market value must be provided by the annuity company, which factors in the value of the death benefit and any other income enhancements.

One other point pertains to IRA annuities that have been annuitized. If the IRA is annuitized (where you receive a stated monthly income from an annuity) it cannot be used to satisfy the RMD requirements from other IRA accounts. If you have annuity investments in your IRA, discuss your distribution options with your financial advisor or tax professional.

Roth IRA

The Roth IRA does not require an RMD when the account owner turns 70 ½. The Roth IRA can continue to grow, tax deferred. When the account owner passes away, the beneficiary must start taking RMDs. We'll look at beneficiary RMDs next.

Beneficiary IRA

The beneficiary IRA can be either a traditional IRA or a Roth IRA. RMDs must be taken from the beneficiary IRA account or a 50 percent penalty will apply to the required amount not withdrawn by the beneficiary. The RMD is impacted by how old the IRA account owner was at her/his date of death. This is covered in greater detail in the next chapter.

Unlike a traditional IRA, the custodian is not required to give the beneficiary an RMD notice.

Spousal IRA and Payroll Deducted IRA

Spousal and payroll deducted IRAs can be either traditional IRA or Roth IRAs. The RMD rules follow the RMD rules described above for these IRA types.

Rollover IRA
This form of IRA follows the traditional IRA RMD rules noted above.

Employer-Funded Retirement Plans

Simplified Employee Pension Plan (SEP IRA)
RMDs apply to SEP IRA accounts. The RMD must be taken when the account owner turns 70 ½, even if he or she is still employed and the employer is still making annual contributions The RMD generally will be less than the annual contribution being made by the employer. The individual, not the employer, is responsible for making sure a distribution is taken. The calculation is the same as discussed under traditional IRAs—take the prior year's December 31 ending account balance and divide it by the account owner's current-year life expectancy.

Since the SEP IRA is a type of IRA, the distributions from the IRAs and SEP IRAs can be aggregated and taken from any one of an account holder's IRA accounts or from more than one account. Furthermore, like the traditional IRA, these distributions are considered ordinary income and subject to federal income tax. Check with your tax advisor about any state tax implications.

Profit-Sharing Plan
If you have a profit-sharing plan, an RMD must be taken. However, if you're 70 ½ or older and still employed, you may be allowed to delay taking the RMD until April 1, of the year following the year of separation from service. This exception must be supported by a provision in the plan document. The ability to delay distributions until the year following the year of separation will require two distributions in the same year. Again, this larger distribution can be avoided by taking a distribution in the year of separation. The ability to delay distributions is not available to 5 percent or more business owners or their family members, and it only applies when the plan document has this special language. The RMD must be taken from each retirement plan and cannot be aggregated with RMDs from IRA accounts or other qualified retirement plans.

Regarding the profit-sharing plan and all the other retirement plans discussed, the federal income tax implications follow the IRA rules. That is, even RMDs are considered ordinary income. As such, they are subject to federal income tax. A discussion with a tax advisor is recommended concerning state income tax considerations.

Money Purchase Pension Plan

A money purchase pension plan has the same requirements as the profit-sharing plan. Like the profit-sharing plan, the RMD must be taken from each retirement plan and cannot be aggregated with IRA accounts or other qualified retirement accounts. Also, distributions are subject to federal income tax. A discussion with a tax advisor is recommended concerning state tax implications.

> For example, if Linda has a money purchase plan, a profit-sharing plan, and a traditional IRA account, she would need to take an RMD from each of the three accounts once she reached 70 ½. Each account will have the RMD calculation made based on their respective December 31 ending balance and divided by Linda's life expectancy. The money purchase pension plan may allow the individual who continues to work after reaching 70 ½ to delay distributions until separation from service. Remember, this special ability to delay distributions does not apply to a 5 percent or more business owner or his or her family members.

Stock Bonus Plan

A stock bonus plan will either be a profit-sharing plan or money purchase pension plan. The plan document will identify whether distributions could be delayed until the individual has separated from service. Remember, this special ability to delay distributions does not apply to a 5 percent or more business owner or that individual's family members. Also, the plan may allow the individual to take in-kind distributions of company stock. It is best to speak with the plan administrator regarding the plan distribution provisions.

Target Benefit Plan

A target benefit plan is a type of pension plan and will follow the money purchase pension plan rules for RMDs.

Defined Benefit Plan

The defined benefit plan, too, is a type of pension plan. Check the plan document for specific details.

- RMDs must be taken when you the account owner turns age 70 ½.
- Distributions can be delayed until separation from service; this caveat doesn't apply to 5 percent or more business owners and their family members.
- There is a 50 percent penalty for not taking the RMD or taking less than the required annual amount.
- RMDs cannot be aggregated with other retirement plan or IRA distributions.

Cash Balance Plan

Since the cash balance plan is a type of defined benefit plan, it follows the defined benefit plan distribution requirements.

Fully Insured Defined Benefit Plans: 412(e) Plan

The 412(e) is a type of defined benefit plan and follows the defined benefit plan distribution rules. Distributions must be taken after the individual has attained age 70 ½ or after the individual has separated from service, whichever is later. This ability to delay RMDs does not apply to 5 percent or more business owners and their immediate family members.

Employee-Funded Retirement Plans (Salary Deferral Plans)

SIMPLE IRA

The SIMPLE IRA follows the distribution and tax rules outlined for the traditional IRA. This plan does not allow the individual to delay distributions until separation from service, thereby requiring a distribution following the attainment of age 70 ½. The SIMPLE RMD can be aggregated with other IRA RMDs and taken from any or all of the IRA accounts.

SARSEP

Like the SIMPLE IRA, the SARSEP follows the rules outlined for the traditional IRA. This plan requires distributions after attaining age 70 ½; there is no special provision to delay distributions until separation from service. The SARSEP RMD can be aggregated with other IRA RMDs and taken from any or all of the IRA accounts.

Traditional 401(k) and Safe Harbor 401(k) Plans

Either plan may have special language that allows an individual who is still employed to delay distributions. Each plan allows someone still working to both receive contributions as well as delay taking distributions. A 5 percent or more business owner and family members must start taking distributions once they reach 70 ½, even if they are still employed. RMDs cannot be aggregated with other plans or IRA distributions.

For federal income tax purposes, distributions follow the tax rules discussed under traditional IRAs. State tax implications should be discussed with a tax advisor.

403(b) or Tax-Sheltered Annuity (TSA)

This plan may have special language to delay the distributions past 70 ½. Check with the plan administrator or the plan document. Some basic rules include the following:

- RMDs cannot be aggregated with other plans or IRA distributions.
- Distributions can be delayed until separation from service (because these entities don't have business owners, the 5 percent or more owner and family member restriction does not apply).
- There is a 50 percent penalty for not taking the RMD or taking less than the required annual amount.
- Distributions are considered ordinary income subject to federal income tax; state tax rules vary by state and should be discussed with a tax advisor.

457(b) Plan

This plan may have special language to delay distributions past age 70 ½. Check with the plan administrator or the plan document. These plans also follow these rules:

- RMDs cannot be aggregated with other plans or IRA distributions.
- Distributions can be delayed until separation from service (as with the 403(b) plan, these business entities don't have business owners, so the 5 percent or more owner and family member restriction does not apply).

- There is a 50 percent penalty for not taking the RMD or taking less than the required annual amount.
- Distributions are considered ordinary income subject to federal income tax; state tax rules vary by state and should be discussed with a tax advisor.

Other Types of Retirement Plans

Employer Stock Ownership Plan (ESOP)
This plan also may have special language to delay distributions past age 70 ½. Check with the plan administrator or the plan document.

Nonqualified Deferred Compensation Plan
Since this plan is not a qualified retirement plan, it doesn't require distributions when the individual reaches 70 ½. The plan will direct how and when distributions start.

Summary
The following chart summarizes the distribution rules for each plan type.

Feature	Traditional IRA	Roth IRA	SEP IRA	Profit Sharing	Defined Benefit	SIMPLE IRA	401(k)	403(b)
Subject to Early Withdrawal penalty	Yes	Only applies to earnings when non-qualified distribution	Yes	Yes	Yes	Yes	Yes	Yes
Withdrawals restricted to specified event: death, disability, retirement, or separation from service	No	No	No	Yes	Yes	No	Yes	Yes
Delay RMDs after attaining age 70½ until separation from service	No	Yes, not required during life of account owner	No	Yes	Yes	No	Yes	Yes
RMDs required from each account	Can aggregate with other IRAs	Not required during life of account owner	Can aggregate with other IRAs	Yes	Yes	Can aggregate with other IRAs	Yes	Yes
Distributions taxed as ordinary income at Federal level	Yes	Only applies to earnings when non-qualified distribution	Yes	Yes	Yes	Yes	Yes	Yes
Distributions taxed by state	consult with tax advisor	consult with tax advisor	consult with tax advisor	consult with tax advisor	consult with tax advisor	consult with tax advisor	consult with tax advisor	consult with tax advisor

CHAPTER 8:
DISTRIBUTIONS AND TAX IMPLICATIONS UPON AN ACCOUNT OWNER'S DEATH

Chapter 7 focused on distribution rules while the account owner was alive. Those distribution rules were classified as premature distributions, which are distributions taken prior to attaining age 59 ½; normal distributions, which are distributions taken after attaining age 59 ½ and prior to attaining age 70 ½; and Required Minimum Distributions, which are distributions required to be taken after attaining age 70 ½. Now, in this chapter we discuss how distributions are taken from the retirement account after the account owner passes away.

The following distribution and tax rules are identical for all the plan types we've discussed. However, nonqualified deferred compensation plans are governed by contract law. Therefore, their distributions do not follow these rules; rather, they will follow the terms of the contract at the death of the individual account owner. There are also some differences that apply to Roth IRAs; these are noted in the text.

Premature Distribution Penalty

As you learned in chapter 7, there are several exceptions to the premature distribution penalty. One exception to the 10 percent early withdrawal penalty pertains to distributions by a beneficiary necessitated because of the account owner's death. These rules can be challenging, and seeking assistance from your financial advisor or tax professional is recommended.

Death Distributions

One of two sets of distribution rules must be followed by beneficiaries after the account owner's passing. Which set must be followed is based on whether the account owner passes away before or after attaining his or her Required Beginning Date, which is April 1 of the year following the year the account owner turns 70 ½. For simplicity, we'll use "pre-" and "post-" 70 ½ to describe these rules.

Pre–70 ½

When the account owner passes away prior to the Required Beginning Date, the beneficiary, including the estate, can keep the account, tax-deferred, by changing the account to a beneficiary IRA. All beneficiaries have the following two options:

1. Start distributions by December 31 of the year following the year of the account owner's death, based on the beneficiary's life expectancy
2. Withdraw the entire account balance by December 31 of the fifth anniversary of the account owner's death

If the primary beneficiary is the spouse, the surviving spouse can utilize one of the above rules. However, the surviving spouse, and only the surviving spouse as beneficiary, has two additional alternatives. The surviving spouse has the ability to:

1. Roll the money to his or her own retirement account, taking distributions when the account owner (surviving spouse) turns 70 ½
2. Leave the money in beneficiary IRA form and start taking distributions when the deceased account holder would have turned age 70 ½; RMDs are based on the younger spouse's life expectancy

Each situation is different, so you should speak with your financial advisor or tax professional.

In the case of many qualified retirement plans—401(k), profit sharing, etc.—the entire account should be directly transferred to a beneficiary IRA to keep the assets tax-deferred and allow the beneficiary to take distributions over his or her lifetime. Each beneficiary should check the plan's document for details.

Remember, the beneficiary can always take out more money than the calculations require.

Post–70 ½

When the account owner passes away after the Required Beginning Date, the beneficiary's options are reduced. The first two options apply to all beneficiaries (spouse and non-spouse). The third option applies only to a spouse as beneficiary:

1. The beneficiary must take the distributions starting December 31 of the year following the account owner's death, based on the single life expectancy of the beneficiary, unless the beneficiary is the estate. If the estate is the beneficiary, the distributions will be based on the single life expectancy of the deceased account owner.

2. The five-year rule, where distributions are not required annually, is no longer an option. However, the distributions can be taken out more quickly than single life expectancy. Beneficiaries can take a lump-sum withdrawal, which would satisfy the distribution requirements. Otherwise, the beneficiary may start with single life distributions, but as additional amounts are needed, he or she may take additional amounts without incurring a penalty.

3. Like the pre–70 ½ rules, a surviving spouse can roll the money to his or her own IRA account and begin distributions when he or she reaches age 70 ½; the spouse may also elect to leave the account in beneficiary form and continue to take distributions in the same fashion as the deceased account owner. A non-spouse beneficiary cannot roll the money to his or her own account but can move it directly to a beneficiary IRA account reflecting the name of the deceased owner; this will keep the money tax-deferred.

What are the consequences to the beneficiary of not taking the RMD? Essentially, the penalty to the beneficiary for not taking the RMD is 50 percent of the amount that should have been withdrawn. If, for example, the RMD was calculated to be $20,000, the penalty for not taking the $20,000 from the account would be $10,000 — in addition to still being required to take the $20,000 RMD. The beneficiary must take distributions during the tax year. There is no ability to extend the distribution deadline.

If payments are taken annually, payment amounts will differ from year to year. The beneficiary can always take more from the account, but not less than the stated annual amount. Beneficiaries can also take a lump-sum distribution, which is the withdrawal of the entire balance within one year. Money can be withdrawn by the beneficiary without the early withdrawal penalty. The early withdrawal penalty does not apply to distributions that are taken, regardless of the age of the beneficiary, because the account owner has passed away.

Beneficiary Designations

Caution should be taken with regard to spousal beneficiaries. If the surviving spouse rolls the money to his or her own IRA (no longer keeping it in beneficiary form) distributions may be subject to the 10 percent early withdrawal penalty if the surviving spouse is under age 59 ½, since he or she is now the account owner.

When it comes to death distributions, it makes sense in many cases for the surviving spouse or other beneficiary to keep the account open as a beneficiary account to avoid the early withdrawal penalty. However, once the spouse as beneficiary reaches age 59 ½, the IRA ownership should be changed to the surviving spouse's name. This will allow the most flexibility in distributions. The surviving spouse as beneficiary can name new beneficiaries to the IRA or retirement plan account, which allows for the longest payouts based on the beneficiary's single life expectancy.

For clarification, let's take a look at some examples.

Pre–70 ½

Peter passed away at age 45. His spouse, Caroline, is the primary beneficiary. Caroline is 42 years of age, doesn't currently need income, but may need income when their children start college. If she leaves Peter's IRA account in beneficiary form with Peter's name as the owner in the account registration, Caroline could start annual distributions by December 31 of the year following Peter's death or delay distributions until Peter would have turned 70 ½. The distributions would be based on Caroline's single life expectancy. When she reaches age 59 ½ or when she no longer has a need for the income, she could change the account title to her name as the IRA owner. This allows her to stop distributions until she turns 70 ½. *Remember*, she can always take out more—but not less—than the annual amount.

In another pre–70 ½ example, Sam passed away at age 67. His surviving spouse, Jill, age 64, is the primary beneficiary. Jill can leave the IRA account in Sam's name and delay taking distributions until Sam would have turned 70 ½, or she could roll the IRA to her own name. By rolling the IRA to her name, Jill would not start RMDs until she turns 70 ½. She must remember, however, to name new beneficiaries on the account.

Post–70 ½

This example concerns Grace, who passed away at age 75. She named Bob and Susan, her children, as primary beneficiaries. It was verified that Grace took her Required Minimum Distribution from her IRA for the year of her death. Since Bob and Susan are required to take distributions, they need to choose the methodology for future distributions. The options are:

1. Both could start distributions by December 31 of the year following Grace's death, based on the oldest beneficiary's life expectancy;
2. The account could be split so that Bob could take distributions based on his life expectancy and Susan could take distributions based on her life expectancy; if they choose this option, the accounts must be split by December 31 of the year following Grace's death in order for Bob and Susan to each use their own single life expectancy in the distribution calculation; or
3. If Bob wants to take a lump sum and Susan wants to take distributions over her life expectancy, Bob should remove his lump sum by September 30 of the year following Grace's death.

Note that Bob and Susan are not spousal beneficiaries. They will need to establish their IRAs in beneficiary form, which means leaving Grace as the account owner with the account showing for the benefit of (fbo) Bob and/or Susan. If you are in a similar situation, check with the IRA custodian on how to establish the accounts in beneficial form.

Federal income tax applies to death distributions. Death distributions are handled like normal distributions. All death distributions are taxed as ordinary income. With regard to state income tax, you should consult with a tax professional.

Roth IRA Distributions

As mentioned in chapter 1, the Roth IRA allows for tax-free distributions of both the contributions and earnings. Unlike the rules for the traditional IRA, when the Roth IRA account owner dies, the rules are simplified. There is no post–70 ½ rule. All Roth death distributions are treated as if the Roth IRA account owner died prior to age 70 ½. So, to reiterate:

When the Roth IRA account owner passes away (regardless of age), the beneficiary, including the estate, can keep the account tax-deferred by changing the account to a beneficiary Roth IRA. All beneficiaries have the following two options:

1. Start distributions by December 31 of the year following the year of the account owner's death, based on the beneficiary's life expectancy
2. Withdraw the entire balance by December 31 of the fifth year after the account owner's death

If the beneficiary is the estate, the only option is to remove the entire balance by the end of the fifth year following the year of death.

If the primary beneficiary is the spouse, the surviving spouse can utilize one of the above rules. However, the surviving spouse has two additional alternatives. The surviving spouse has the ability to:

1. Roll the money to his or her own Roth IRA account and start taking distributions when he or she turns 70 ½
2. Leave the account in beneficiary Roth IRA form and start taking distributions when the deceased account holder would have turned 70 ½

There are two differences with Roth IRA death distributions that must be identified:

1. The Roth IRA account must be held for five years in order for the distribution to be tax-free
2. The non-spouse beneficiary of a traditional IRA cannot do a conversion to a beneficiary Roth IRA; however, a spouse can convert a deceased spouse's traditional IRA to a Roth IRA in his or her own name. This would be a taxable event

As with the traditional IRA, the beneficiary of a Roth IRA can take out more money than the required amount. Also, beneficiaries should name new beneficiaries on the account.

Careful consideration should be taken on any withdrawals before the five-year holding period has been met by the deceased account holder. This is because earnings withdrawn from the Roth conversion account that have not been held in the account for five years from the date of the conversion will be taxable. The 10 percent early withdrawal penalty would not apply, since distributions are required due to death of the account holder.

Let's look at an example of how the five-year rule would work in the case of Ted. Ted passed away in 2012. He had made contributions to his Roth IRA in 2010 and 2011, so the Roth IRA was only in place for three years prior to his passing. If his daughter, Cindy, takes a total distribution of the Roth account by December 31, 2013, she will incur taxes only on the earnings, since the account hasn't been open for five years. Ted's contributions (which were made in 2010 and 2011) would be considered cost basis, because he didn't take a tax deduction when the contributions were originally made to the account. Remember, Roth contributions are not tax deductible. A total distribution made to Cindy would include Ted's cost basis, which is not taxable to Cindy, along with any earnings accrued on the investment within the account. In order for the Roth IRA distribution to be tax-free to Cindy, the account must be open for five years. In this case, the account was only open for three years. Cindy would not be subject to the 10 percent early withdrawal penalty because the distribution is after Ted's death. However, she would be taxed on the earnings.

If she wants to receive the distribution without incurring federal income tax, Cindy has two options:

1. She could leave the account in beneficiary form for two years after Ted's passing, completing the five-year holding period. Because Roth IRA distributions always have the five-year RMD option, Cindy is not obligated to take a withdrawal until the fifth year following Ted's death. By not taking a distribution for two years, Cindy satisfies Ted's five-year holding period, thus making the distribution a qualified distribution, since it was held for five years and distributed due to Ted's death. This strategy would allow Cindy to take tax-free distributions from Ted's Roth IRA.
2. She could leave the account in beneficiary form and start taking distributions by December 31, 2013 based on her single life expectancy. After the five-

year holding period has been met, she could elect to take a full withdrawal from the account (taking the distribution quicker) or she can continue to take distributions over her life expectancy. As with the first case, she wouldn't pay any federal income tax, since the distributions are qualified distributions.

The next example is about Ben. Ben is the son of JoAnna, who recently passed away. He is the primary beneficiary on JoAnna's Roth IRA account. Since JoAnna started her Roth IRA in 2005, JoAnna met the five-year holding requirement. Ben would be able to take distributions from JoAnna's Roth IRA without paying federal income tax and without paying penalty on the entire distribution. Ben has met the rules to take tax-free distributions, which is described as a qualified Roth distribution.

The Roth IRA is a great way to pass an inheritance to a designated beneficiary without the beneficiary incurring federal income tax. Also, since the Roth IRA passes directly to the beneficiary, as do all tax-deferred accounts, it bypasses the probate process. The Roth IRA is part of the taxable estate, but it passes directly to the named beneficiary as do all tax-deferred retirement accounts.

Retirement Plan Distributions

Some retirement plans of employers require that distributions be taken by December 31 of the year following the year of death or within a stated period after the death of the individual employee. Generally, several options are available:

1. The plan will allow the distributions to be direct rolled to a beneficiary IRA in the case of a non-spouse beneficiary. A direct rollover occurs when the distribution is sent between financial institutions without receipt by the beneficiary.
2. The plan will allow the distributions to be rolled over to the surviving spouse's IRA account.
3. The money might be allowed to remain in the retirement plan, but the account will be re-titled to the name of the beneficiary.

Rollovers

If you are a non-spouse beneficiary of an IRA or other retirement plan, you cannot take the withdrawal from the account and redeposit the money within sixty days to an IRA or your own retirement plan. In this case, if you don't want the money to be taxed currently, directly roll the money to a beneficiary IRA. We recommend that you name a subsequent beneficiary on the account to receive payments, in the event you pass away before the entire account has been distributed. You have the ability to name a new primary and contingent beneficiary to take over the payments.

When doing a direct rollover, the money is paid from the IRA custodian or plan trustee directly to the beneficiary IRA. If you, as the non-spouse beneficiary, received a check from the retirement plan or IRA custodian, once it's been issued and deposited, it can no longer be reapplied as a beneficiary IRA or put back into a tax-deferred retirement account. If this has happened, you can look at alternatives, such as investing in a tax-deferred account or making your annual IRA contribution. Your IRA contribution will be limited to $5,500 if you are under 50 or $6,500 if you are 50 or over (2013 limits). Also, remember that the IRA contribution might be limited based on your participation in a retirement plan at work and your Adjusted Gross Income (AGI).

We've only addressed the impacts of a spouse or a non-spouse being named as beneficiary on the retirement account(s). If the account owner named a trust, estate, charity, or other non-person as the beneficiary of any of the retirement plans discussed in this book, beneficiaries should consult a tax advisor and estate attorney to determine how this designation impacts the distributions from the IRA or retirement plan(s).

Additional Considerations

Hindsight is 20/20; foresight is unclear. But in this case, not naming a beneficiary or not reviewing beneficiary designations is a serious oversight. We recommend reviewing beneficiary designations whenever a life event occurs: death or birth of a family member, marriage of a family member, divorce, changing jobs, etc. Naming a beneficiary should be given the same amount of consideration as choosing the amount to contribute annually to the retirement account. This decision will have long-lasting consequences for your loved ones.

Information that is necessary to gather or prepare when the account owner passes away with retirement assets include:

- account owner's age at death;
- beneficiary(ies) listed on the account;
- prior year–ending account balance used for RMD calculations;
- details of account values at date of death;
- if post–70 ½, whether an RMD was taken prior to passing away;
- current investment statements;
- if you keep the account in beneficiary form, name of a subsequent beneficiary, in the event the original beneficiary passes away prior to the entire account being distributed;
- death certificate of account owner; and
- letter of instruction to current custodian, signed by all beneficiaries.

We conclude this chapter by including a list[24] of important documents. These documents have probably been accumulated during your working years but are probably located in a variety of places. Centralize them! Furthermore, as important as it is to maintain such files, your heirs and executors must be aware of their existence and where they can be found. Important documents include:

1. Medical histories;
2. Durable health-care power of attorney;
3. Authorization to release medical information;
4. Living will;
5. Do-not-resuscitate order;
6. Will and trust documents;
7. Life insurance policies;
8. IRAs and other retirement account documents;
9. Pension documents and annuity contracts;
10. List of bank accounts;
11. List of user names and passwords;
12. Safe-deposit box information;
13. Safe information;
14. Real- and personal-property ownership documents;

---

24   Chaudhyri, Saabira. "The Twenty-Five Documents You Need Before You Die." *Wall Street Journal*, July 2–3, 2011.

15. Escrow accounts;
16. Loans and debt instruments;
17. Stock and bond certificates, brokerage account statements;
18. Partnership and corporation papers; and
19. Tax returns.

Summary

The following chart summarizes RMD and tax ramifications upon an account owner's death. Consult a tax advisor regarding state taxation and for guidance regarding client situations.

Feature	Traditional IRA	Roth IRA	SEP IRA	Profit Sharing	Defined Benefit	SIMPLE IRA	401(k)	403(b)
RMD required after account owner passes away	Yes	Yes	Yes	Yes	Yes	Yes	Yes	Yes
Pre/Post-70 ½ rules apply	Yes	Only pre-70 ½ rules apply	Yes	Yes	Yes	Yes	Yes	Yes
Distributions taxed as ordinary income at Federal level	Yes	No, unless not held for 5 years	Yes	Yes	Yes	Yes	Yes	Yes

CHAPTER 9:
RETIREMENT DISTRIBUTION STRATEGIES

While it's easy to withdraw money from retirement accounts, there are strategies that can be used that may help you avoid running out of money. The primary purpose of this chapter is to discuss some time-tested strategies that may be suitable for your personal situation. However, there are some fundamental questions that should be answered before choosing your withdrawal strategy.

How Much Do I Have? How Much Do I Need?

Before using any of the strategies discussed in this chapter, take steps to:

1. Identify the sources of your direct income (i.e., Social Security or Railroad Retirement, income from a defined benefit plan, etc.);
2. Identify other assets that can be used during retirement that generate income, such as individual accounts, rental real estate, outside insurance;
3. Ascertain the value of your retirement plans;
4. Prepare an itemized list of the expenses you may incur if you retired today; and
5. For your estate executors and beneficiaries, keep critical files in an accessible and known location.

The determination of your Social Security or Railroad Retirement benefit is no more complex than making a call to your local administration office or checking either ssa.gov or rrb.gov websites. These websites can also help you determine when you should begin taking benefits. You can begin as early as age sixty-two; however, you would receive only 70 percent of the benefit you would receive at your normal retirement age. Retiring at age 70 offers the maximum benefit achievable. At this point, you would receive approximately 32 percent more benefit than had you started receiving benefits at your normal retirement age. Similarly, if your company offers a defined benefit or other plan that guarantees retirement income, contact the human resources department for retirement income details.

Next, incorporate other sources of income, outside of the "retirement" classification, into your retirement income determination. If you maintain individual investment accounts, rental real estate, or income-generating life insurance, be sure to add this income into your overall retirement income pool.

A determination of how much income you need from your retirement asset pool can be made once you've listed and quantified all the expenses you currently incur and which you expect to incur during retirement. This can be done using a cash flow worksheet, sometimes referred to as a budget. A cash flow worksheet helps you identify and record income and expenses. The preparation of a detailed cash flow is an essential ingredient in your retirement planning process.

When developing your cash flow worksheet, we recommend that you identify your current expenses on a monthly basis. Then we suggest projecting your expected income and expenses for the next five years, using annual estimates. Furthermore, this document should not be viewed as static. When changes occur to income or expenses, which can include projected cost increases, your cash flow worksheet should be updated to reflect those changes. Review your cash flow worksheet at least annually to identify long-term changes or trends in spending habits that may need to be incorporated into your future cash flow worksheets.

An example of a cash flow worksheet is included on the following page. This worksheet would be illustrative of someone sixty-five years of age receiving Social Security benefits, still working, and paying Medicare premiums.

Cash Flow Worksheet

Monthly Sources of Income**

Wages, Salary, Tips (Earned Income)	$ 2,500	
Retirement/Pension Income	$ 2,000	
Dividends and Capital Gain	$ 667	
Interest	$ 250	$3,000 per year
Social Security or Railroad Retirement	$ 2,500	
Defined Pension Benefits	$ 600	
Total Monthly Sources of Income	$ 8,517	

Monthly Uses of Income (Expenditures)**

Food	$ 1,000	
Clothing	$ 400	
Real Estate Tax	$ 375	$4,500 per year
Condominium Fees	$ 850	
Utilities:		
Gas/Electric, Water, Garbage paid by Condominium		
Cable/Internet	$ 25	
Telephone	$ 100	
Gasoline	$ 125	
Automobile Maintenance	$ 100	
Charge Account Payment - vacations and entertainment	$ 1,666	$20,000 per year
Estimate Federal Income Tax Payment	$ 2,000	$6,000 per quarter
Estimate State Income Tax Payment	$ 145	$435 per quarter
Estimated Local Income Tax Payment	$ 100	$300 per quarter
Insurance:		
Medical:		
Medicare A+B and Rx	$ 140	
Supplemental Insurance	$ 200	$600 per quarter
Medicine	$ 350	$420 per year
Home	$ 50	$600 per year
Automobile	$ 166	$2,000 per year
Out-of-Pocket Medical/Dental	$ 42	$500 per year
Club/Association Dues	$ 83	$1,000 per year
Education	$ 250	$3,000 per year
Charitable Contributions	$ 200	$2,400 per year
Other	$ 150	
Total Monthly Uses of Income	$ 8,517	

Surplus/(Deficit)	$0

**If income is received or expenses are paid on a quarterly or other schedule, average the number for a monthly amount. For your specific cash flow other items to consider include:

    Mortgage payment or rent
    Household maintenance and repair
    Automotive or personal loans
    Other transportation expenses
    Life insurance premiums
    Retirement plan contributions

Next, prepare a cash flow worksheet that addresses what income and expenses you expect to continue during your retirement years. While your total amount of income and total expenditures may not be significantly different from your pre-retirement days, the allocations, or from where you are receiving income and spending that income during retirement, may be and probably will be quite different. For example, instead of receiving salaries, you may receive income from your investments and your retirement accounts. During retirement, your expenses shift from work-related expenses to other expenses. You may no longer have an expense for your daily commute and your house may be paid for, but your travel or entertainment expenses may increase. As you slow down on travel, your medical expenses may increase. Your employer-sponsored health and life insurance programs may shift to premiums for Medicare, long-term care, or medigap-type insurance. I think you get the picture.

You should be even more careful when it comes to expenses. The easy expenses to estimate are your fixed ones, such as real estate tax, medical insurance or expenses—Medicare, medigap and Rx, utilities, telephone, TV and Internet, religious and other charitable contributions, car-related gasoline and insurance, home insurance, food, etc. The more difficult expenses to budget are the ones that may or may not happen, such as doctor visits, clothing, entertainment, etc. Err on the side of caution. Be conservative. Jot them down in your projected cash flow worksheet.

Once you have identified and quantified all of your anticipated sources of income and expense (a big task to say the least), the one estimate that remains to be completed is determining the amount of income you should take from your retirement assets.

As a starting point, plan on a 4 percent retirement income stream from your assets. Based on the results of a 1998 Trinity University study conducted by three finance professors, Philip L. Cooley, Carl M. Hubbard, and Daniel T. Walz, it was concluded that withdrawal rates of 3 percent and 4 percent are extremely unlikely to exhaust any portfolio of stocks and bonds. The study back-tested data that covered payout periods from 1925 to 1975.[25] If it's determined, however, that a 4 percent withdrawal rate is insufficient, all is not lost. You may consider using still other assets, if available, or investing differently. (Revisit chapter 3, on types of investments, and chapter 6, for your risk profile.) Also, you may consider delaying your retirement in order to accumulate more retirement principal. Or you may consider part-time employment in a field you love.

Once you have completed your income and expense analysis, the next question to be answered is where you should take the money from.

25 Cooley, Philip L., Carl M. Hubbard and Daniel T. Walz. "Retirement Savings: Choosing a Withdrawal Rate That Is Sustainable." *AAII Journal 10*, 3:16–21, 1998.

From Where Should I Take the Money?

What underlies this question is income taxes. That is, from which type of accounts do you want to initially take distributions: pre-tax dollars (where the distributions are taxable), or after-tax dollars (where the distributions are tax-free).

If your primary concern is to reduce your federal income tax, then your order of distribution should be to liquidate after-tax investment income first and leave the pre-tax investment income for last. If current income tax is not a primary concern, you might consider liquidating just enough pre-tax investment income to keep you in the same tax bracket.

Distribution Strategies to Consider

Below is an overview of five time-tested strategies that have been used to take retirement plan distributions.

1. Pro-rata approach
2. Split-grow-deplete approach
3. Annuity hedge approach
4. Bucket approach
5. Dividend-interest payout approach

Pro-Rata Approach

The pro-rata approach divides your retirement portfolio between equity holdings and fixed income holdings (i.e., bonds). Once a determination is made as to the amount of income you're going to need annually, that income should be withdrawn from your equity and fixed income assets in the same proportions that they are presently allocated.

For example, let's use a hypothetical $300,000 portfolio where 40 percent is in equity and 60 percent is in fixed income. Your annual income need is 4 percent or $12,000. You would take 40 percent or $4,800 from the equity portion and 60 percent or $7,200 from the fixed portion. These withdrawals are a combination of dividends, capital gains, interest, and principal.

	Current portfolio	Income needed	Percent
Equity portion	$120,000	$ 4,800	40%
Fixed Income	$180,000	$ 7,200	60%
Total	$300,000	$12,000	

This strategy can become more complex if you want to reduce your equity portion by type and style of mutual funds held (i.e., large-cap value, mid-cap growth, etc.) in order to maintain the integrity of those relationships. Similarly, the withdrawal from the fixed portion can become more complex if you wish to maintain the relationships of the short-term, intermediate-term, and long-term holdings.

Split-Grow-Deplete Approach

This method is more complex than the pro-rata approach. This method requires that you identify your income need for a specified time period. In the following example, a seven-year time period is used. Initially, you need to identify your income need for the first seven-year cycle. Let's assume your portfolio is $1 million. Your income need is 4 percent or $40,000 annually. Remember, this is an average of your expenses for the next seven years. First, you divide your portfolio into two parts: place $280,000 in your "immediate income need" portfolio ($40,000 for seven years); and place $720,000 in your "growth" portfolio.

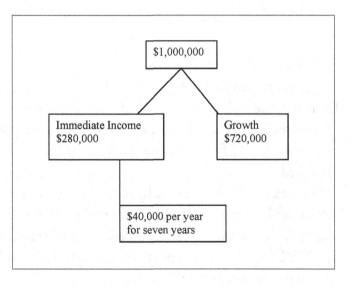

In the "immediate income need" portfolio, your investments should mainly consist of certificates of deposit, Treasury bills, and Treasury notes. The main objective of this portfolio is to guarantee the principal and income; capital growth is not an objective. Conversely, the "growth" portfolio should remain fully invested. The main objective of this portfolio is growth to maintain your purchasing power and remain level with inflation and other cost increases.

In the seventh year, your analysis (done seven years earlier) should be revisited. The remaining portfolio is again split between your immediate income need over the next seven years and the growth portion of the portfolio. Each portion should be invested in a similar manner: the immediate-need portfolio invested into certificates of deposit and treasuries; the growth portion fully invested.

Annuity Hedge Approach

The annuity hedge is an approach where a portion of your investment portfolio is carved out and used to purchase an immediate annuity. This portion would be subject to federal income tax and, possibly, state income tax. This strategy will typically target a guaranteed income of 4 percent annually. One of the limitations of this approach is the size of the portfolio that may be needed to generate the desired income. This approach guarantees an income for life; however, since the amount of income does not change from year to year, purchasing power can diminish. Another limitation of this approach is that you give up control of the amount invested to purchase the annuity.

For example, if your retirement portfolio is $1 million, and you wanted to generate a guaranteed annual income of $40,000 per year, you might need to invest $700,000 or more to purchase that immediate annuity. The remaining amount should be invested in vehicles that at least go to mitigate inflation and other cost increases.

Bucket Approach[26]

The bucket approach is favored by many financial advisors for pre-retirement income savings as well as retirement distribution planning. When using this approach for retirement income, your budget or cash flow worksheet is critical. As with your budget, if you overspend in one area, like an unexpected car expense, you would reduce expenses in another area like entertainment. Within the bucket approach, if you use the short-term bucket quicker than expected, revisit your budget so you can reallocate the income from the buckets. It is not recommended to use the long-term bucket to supplement your short-term needs, since this money is invested for the long-term and subject to higher market volatility than the investments in the short-term bucket. If your short-term bucket isn't being utilized for emergencies or you no longer need as much income from this bucket, you should reallocate the money within the buckets. In this case, short-term money should be moved to the mid-term bucket.

---

26 Banham, Russ. "New Life for an Old Idea: Investment Buckets." *Online.WSJ.com*, 2/8/2012.

The way the bucket approach works is to segregate your retirement portfolio into several "buckets" based on income need that's delineated by time-frame parameters. Typically there are three buckets:

1. Short-term bucket
2. Mid-term bucket
3. Long-term bucket

The **short-term bucket** contains the money necessary for emergencies or unexpected expenses. Short-term funds can be placed in this bucket to supplement your income needs, if necessary. Income from retirement plans, Social Security, or other sources as outlined in your cash flow worksheet will be used for everyday expenses. This funding duration could be from six months to five years, based on your and your financial advisor's preference. Since this is a short-term investment bucket, the objective should be principal preservation. The recommended investments may include cash, bank certificates of deposit, insured money market funds, Treasury bills, and Treasury notes.

The **mid-term bucket** contains money needed over an interim time frame; again, this is your and your financial advisor's preference but typically is a five-year period. The time frame for this bucket is laddered based on the time frame for the short-term bucket. For example, if your short-term bucket is five years, the mid-term bucket would be invested for five to ten years. If the short-term bucket is three years, the mid-term bucket would be three to eight years. This is the bucket that contains the investments that will generate the income for your retirement. If your mid-term period is three years or longer, the primary objective of this money should be principal preservation and income. The mid-term investment bucket would include Treasury notes, corporate bonds, unit investment trust, fixed annuities, and conservatively allocated mutual funds. If your short-term bucket period is less than a three-year period, then this bucket should be a blend of both conservative principal preservation investments, which is the objective for the short-term bucket, and the income-generation objective for this bucket.

The **long-term bucket** contains that portion of your investment portfolio not needed for current income. Think of this as the bucket that has a longer investment time frame greater than the mid-term bucket. For example, if your mid-term bucket is ten years, then the long-term bucket will be invested for a period longer than ten years. It generally contains investments that have a primary objective of conservative growth.

This bucket may include mutual funds, laddered bonds, dividend paying stocks, and rental real estate.

Let's assume your portfolio is $500,000. Your income need is $20,000 annually. This income need is in addition to income from Social Security or other income outlined in your cash flow worksheet. We'll place $70,000 in the short-term bucket, which is $20,000 for three years as well as an additional $10,000 for emergencies. The amount in this bucket held for emergencies is discretionary and can be lower or higher depending on your cash flow worksheet. Also, remember that the holding period is based on your comfort level. Again, in this example, this bucket is for additional expenses for the next three years and emergencies. The next bucket is our mid-term bucket, which will hold the income necessary for the next five years. We put $100,000 in the mid-term bucket. In the last bucket, our long-term bucket, we put in the remaining $330,000.

Short-term	Mid-term	Long-term
$70,000	$100,000	$330,000

Dividend-Interest Payout Approach

This approach divides your retirement portfolio into two categories: an emergency fund category and an income-generating category.

1. Emergency Fund

   This category should contain funds that are only used to meet unforeseen contingencies. It should cover, at a minimum, six months of essential expenses, though, ideally, it should cover closer to two years of expenses. The sole purpose of this account is principal preservation. As such, it should be invested in government-insured certificates of deposit, Treasury bills, and government-insured money market funds.

2. Income-Generating

   This category should contain the bulk of your retirement portfolio. Its purpose is to help generate the income necessary to meet your retirement needs. Since inflation erodes the purchasing power, over time, of fixed income investments, a significant portion of these retirement dollars should be invested in dividend-paying stock mutual funds, dividend-paying ETFs, and the common stocks of high-quality, dividend-paying companies with a history of annual dividend distribution increases. This part of the portfolio will be subject to principal fluctuation; however, this should have no adverse impact on the dividends distributed. The remaining portion of the portfolio should be invested in fixed-income instruments that call for periodic interest income payments and the repayment of the instrument's face value at maturity. These investments may include Treasury notes and bonds, high-quality corporate bonds, high-quality municipal bonds, and possibly an immediate annuity. (An immediate annuity, however, has no maturity date. In fact, ownership of the underlying investment principal is transferred to the insurance company in exchange for a guaranteed lifetime of fixed income payments.)

Summary

The primary purpose of this chapter was to discuss distribution strategies that may be suitable for your personal situation. However, before deciding on a strategy that is most appropriate to meet your needs, several fundamental questions need to be thought about and answered. These questions are:

1. How much do I have?
2. How much do I need?
3. From where should I take the money?
4. How do I take the money?

Once these questions are thoughtfully answered, selecting a distribution strategy should be a lot easier. That said, we just couldn't conclude this chapter without some words on suggested actions that should be taken over the course of your lifetime to assure yourself that you have control of the financial components of your retirement.

We have compiled a list of recommended actions that should be taken during various stages of your adult life. The recommended actions table, on the next page, identifies actions that should be implemented during specified time periods: annually, every five years, between eighteen and twenty-five years of age, between twenty-five and fifty years of age, between fifty and seventy years of age, and at retirement. We hope you find this table useful. Use it as a constant reminder of what needs to be done to help you have a successful retirement.

Recommended Actions

Time Frame	Action
Annually	<ul><li>Reallocate your investment portfolio.</li><li>Verify your Social Security or Railroad Retirement earnings record.</li><li>Make certain financial papers are readily accessible, but secure and in a location which has been communicated to key family members or person handling your final affairs.</li><li>Prepare a monthly cash flow projection (a budget) and follow it!!!</li></ul>
Every Five-Years or a Life Changing Event	<ul><li>Review your beneficiary designations.</li><li>Re-examine and update your will.</li><li>Re-evaluate your insurance coverage.</li><li>Re-assess cash flow projections.</li></ul>
Just Starting Out (age 18-25)	<ul><li>Build an emergency fund to cover essential expenses for 6 months.</li><li>Pay off student loans and credit cards to establish a credit score.</li><li>Start a savings program by funding an IRA, contributing to your retirement plan at work or opening a savings account. Start putting away 3% of pay, increasing this 1% annually (as you can afford it) to attain a savings rate of 10%.</li><li>Purchase insurance either through your employer or individually. Consult with your financial advisor regarding coverage, types and amounts. Purchase a base amount of cash value life insurance; supplement it with 30-year level term insurance. Your goal should be to cover your liabilities to avoid leaving your heirs with debt.</li><li>Have a will prepared, include a power of attorney and medical power of attorney.</li></ul>
Earning Years (age 25-50)	Continue your good habits established during your "Just Starting Out Years." As your earnings increase, consider these action items:<ul><li>Expand your emergency fund to cover one-two years of essential expenses.</li><li>Increase your contributions to your retirement plans and start saving for your children's education.</li><li>Protect your real property interests by purchasing umbrella liability and homeowner's insurance.</li><li>Purchase disability and long-term care insurance, either through your employer or individually.</li><li>Develop interests that will last a lifetime.</li></ul>
Pre–Retirement Years (age 50–70)	Continue your "Earning Years" actions. As you approach retirement, consider these action items:<ul><li>Start planning for retirement by determining the amount of money you may need at retirement. Are you on track?</li><li>Five years prior to your anticipated retirement date, start re-positioning your assets to a more conservative or income producing portfolio.</li></ul>
Retirement Years	<ul><li>Reposition your investments and other assets to generate needed retirement income.</li><li>Pursue your avocational interests that have been developed over time.</li><li>Consider life style changes during retirement; such as downsizing living quarters, assisted care, moving closer to family, etc.</li><li>Organize your legacy plan–get your legal and medical papers in order, make certain your will reflects your wishes, establish a trust if desired, develop gifting strategies; make funeral and burial arrangements, etc.</li></ul>

CONCLUSION

Retirement, that inevitable phase of one's life cycle, will be upon you before you know it. Ladies, are you ready? Even if you believe you're ready, we hope this book has provided added value and insight into the retirement plan(s) you and (possibly) your partner have, and answered questions even the human resources department at your firm didn't know.

Just being able to see a readable description of the plan(s) you have was, we hope, worth the time you spent reading *Women & Retirement Planning: Understanding Retirement Plans, Investment Choices, and Retirement Plan Distributions.* But when these descriptions were augmented in chapter 2 with information on contribution limits and critical contribution deadlines, we wouldn't be surprised if this was the first time you saw such information in a descriptive, easy-to-read, and understandable form. We hope this gave you that "wow" moment that inspired you to read on.

As you probably know, the bedrock of any retirement is what you put into it. We introduced an array of basic investment alternatives available to you. While emphasizing mutual funds, we described the primary advantages and disadvantages of a variety of investment alternatives. In addition to mutual funds, we highlighted exchange traded funds, closed-end funds, common and preferred stock, Treasury securities, municipal and corporate bonds, unit investment trusts (UIT), annuities, and real estate.

We emphasized mutual funds for several reasons. First and foremost was the understanding that this is the most widely used investment option for IRAs, employer-funded retirement plans, and employee-funded retirement plans. Second, mutual funds provide immediate diversification and thereby have a tendency to reduce volatility. Third, mutual funds provide a simple means to allocate your investments. Mutual funds also provide professional management at a modest cost. And the transaction cost associated with a mutual fund is small or even zero.

In emphasizing mutual funds, we also discussed a process for selecting those mutual funds best suited for you. Although the discussion was abbreviated when compared to the discourse in Don's book, *Women & Mutual Funds: Gain Understanding and Be in Control*, it was deemed important to highlight the key statistical factors used in the selection process. The factors described were percentile rank in category, standard deviation, beta and R^2, and alpha.

Then, of course, we returned to that inevitable phase of one's life cycle: retirement. This time, in our discussion on distributions, we tried to distinguish the mandated or Required Minimum Distribution (RMD) from the voluntary distribution within IRA plans (traditional, Roth, beneficiary, spousal, and rollover), employer-funded plans, such as a SEP, profit-sharing, money purchase and defined benefit plans, and salary deferral plans that include the SIMPLE IRA, 401(k), or 403(b).

The unique aspect of RMDs is that an account owner must begin taking these distributions from a retirement plan (excluding a Roth IRA) by April 1 after attaining age 70 ½. And, after that milestone is reached, distributions must be taken every year thereafter based upon your remaining life expectancy.

Generally, there are exceptions to rules; the rule that governs Required Minimum Distributions is no exception. It's important to understand that the rules are different when working with an account owner as opposed to working with a beneficiary. Distributions upon the account owner's death fall into two categories: pre–70 ½ distributions and post–70 ½ distributions. Then we talked about necessary distributions from a Roth IRA. It is important to know that distributions from a Roth IRA are not required until the account owner's death and follow the distribution rules of "pre–70 ½."

The preparation of a detailed cash flow is an essential ingredient in your retirement planning process. (A sample of a cash flow worksheet is included in chapter 9.) The purpose of a cash flow is to show from where you'll be receiving income and on what you plan or need to spend your income. Preparation of this inventory should not be taken lightly, and you should delegate some time to compile your sources of income and your expenditures.

A critical follow-up to your cash flow worksheet is the selection of a distribution strategy or strategies that give you that level of comfort and assurance that you'll not outlive your money. Perhaps your selected strategy is the pro-rata approach, or it could be the split-grow-deplete method; or maybe it's the annuity hedge approach, the bucket approach, or possibly the dividend-income payout approach. Whichever approach you choose, whether from one or more of the above-mentioned strategies—or some other one—we wish you the very best.

Throughout the book, we placed special emphasis on seeking guidance from a financial advisor and tax professional. It's that important! Having financial experts help you navigate through the complexities of financial decision making will be hugely beneficial. You may not feel a need for this additional help when you are starting out, but as your assets grow, your financial situation becomes more complex, your personal time becomes less your own, and you can afford the additional expense, invest your time and money in professional advice. Professional advice is an integral part of our list of recommended actions to implement throughout your adult life.

Finally, we hope you found *Women & Retirement Planning: Understanding Retirement Plans, Investment Choices, and Retirement Plan Distributions* informative and that you make it a permanent part of your reference library. We wish this book could focus on your specific retirement issues. In that way, we would be certain that you would be doing the right thing about understanding and controlling your retirement plan distributions. Unfortunately, it is not possible to do that within the context of this book. What we attempted to do, however, was to provide detailed information and illustrations about all available retirement options. In that way, you are able to select those options that fit your profile and develop and implement your strategy. If, after reading this book, you're still uncomfortable about using the information and developing your approach and strategy, please consult with your tax professional or financial advisors. We wish you good fortune and a financially secure retirement!

ABOUT THE AUTHORS

Donald S. Gudhus, MBA, is the founder and president of Oracle Financial Group. Founded in 1993 and located in Center City Philadelphia, Oracle Financial Group is a Registered Investment Advisor. The firm offers a complete array of financial services but is primarily focused on investment management for individual and retirement accounts.

Don is the author of the well-received book on mutual funds, *Women & Mutual Funds: Gain Understanding and Be in Control.* Published in 2008, this book offers a methodology for analyzing and selecting mutual funds and creating a portfolio as well as suggestions about monitoring and adjusting the portfolio when necessary.

Don's business experience began in private industry with companies such as RCA-Hertz and Consolidated Rail Corporation, where he directed the operating and capital budgeting functions. His first entrepreneurial venture was in 1993, when he founded Oracle Financial Group.

Don's education includes a BBA in finance and economics and an MBA in financial management from Pace University in New York City. He completed his US Army active duty obligation at Fort Polk, Louisiana. Don is also a graduate of the CFP® Professional Education Program from the College for Financial Planning in Denver, Colorado. Don is a member of the Philadelphia Securities Association and has been named in *Philadelphia Magazine* by Five Star Professional, a top wealth manager in the Philadelphia area for 2010, 2011, and 2012. He has also lectured on investing at the Community College of Philadelphia as well as other venues.

Donald S. Gudhus and Oracle Financial Group do not provide legal advice. Please consult your tax, financial planning, and legal advisors before implementing an investment strategy or retirement plan.

Carol J. Ventura, MBA, CFP®, CLU, ChFC, CEBS, RPA, GBA, is the retirement services manager for H.D. Vest Financial Services®, located in Irving, Texas. Carol focuses on retirement plan design and training. She has made presentations on qualified plans, lump-sum distributions, employee benefit plans, educational funding, year-end tax planning, buy-sell agreements, risk analysis, and tax credit programs. She has published articles for *Tax Pro Journal*, Wells Fargo Connections, and Financial Planning Focus for the American Society of CLU and ChFC. She has been a featured speaker for the Texas Society of CPAs satellite broadcast and Wells Fargo Small Business Webcast.

Carol received her BS in business administration and her MBA from the University of Wisconsin-LaCrosse. Carol is a CFP® professional, certified life underwriter (CLU), chartered financial consultant (ChFC), certified employee benefit specialist (CEBS), retirement plans associate (RPA), and group benefits associate (GBA). She is a member of the Financial Planning Association, Society of Financial Service Professionals, and the International Foundation of Employee Benefit Plans.

The views and opinions are not those of H.D. Vest Financial Services® (H.D. Vest) or its subsidiaries. Investment opinions and related information presented reflect those solely of Don Gudhus.

The information is provided for educational purposes only. H.D. Vest Financial Services® and its affiliates do not provide legal advice. Please consult your legal advisors to determine how this information may apply to your own situation. H.D. Vest Financial Services® or its affiliates do not provide tax advice. Whether any planned tax result is realized by you depends on the specific facts of your situation at the time your tax preparer submits your tax return.

The information presented is not an offer to buy or sell, or a solicitation of any offer to buy or sell the securities or implement the strategies mentioned. The investments discussed or recommended in the material may be unsuitable for some investors depending on their specific investment objectives and financial position. Investors should consult with their financial advisor or tax professional regarding their specific situation.

REFERENCES

Banham, Russ. "New Life for an Old Idea: Investment Buckets." ONLINE.WSJ.com, 2/8/12.

Beebower, Gilbert, Michael Hogan, and Robert Ludwig. "Asset Allocation: Is It a Hoax?" SEI, Spring 1998.

Brinson, Gary P., Randolph Hood, and Gilbert L. Beebower. "Determinants of Portfolio Performance." *Financial Analysts Journal,* July/August 1986.

Brinson, Gary P., Brian D. Singer, Gilbert L. Beebower. "Determinants of Portfolio Performance II: An Update." *Financial Analysts Journal,* May/June 1991.

Calhoun, Carol V., and Arthur H. Tepler. "Deferred Retirement Option Plans (DROP Plans)." *Pension and Benefits Week,* October 13, 1998.

Chaudhyri, Saabira. "The Twenty-Five Documents You Need Before You Die." *Wall Street Journal,* July 2–3, 2011.

Choosing a Retirement Solution for Your Small Business. IRS Publication 3998.

Cooley, Philip L., Carl M. Hubbard, and Daniel T. Walz. "Retirement Savings: Choosing a Withdrawal Rate That Is Sustainable." *AAII Journal,* 10, 3:16–21, 1998.

Darst, David M. *The Art of Asset Allocation.* New York: McGraw-Hill Companies, 2003.

Deferred Retirement Option Programs. VanKampen. Seminar, 2004.

Duska, Ronald F., PhD. "On Helping Your Retirees." *Journal of Financial Service Professionals*, January 2011.

Evensky, Harold. "The Hoax Is a Hoax." *Financial Planning*, November 1997.

"Financial Experience & Behaviors among Women: 2010–2011." Prudential Research Study. Newark, NJ: The Prudential Insurance Company of America. Tenth Anniversary Edition, 2010.

Gudhus, Donald S. *Women & Mutual Funds: Gain Understanding and Be in Control*. Bloomington, IN: iUniverse, 2008.

Ibbotson, Roger G., and Paul D. Kaplan. "Does Asset Allocation Policy Explain 40, 90, or 100 Percent of Performance?" Available at www.ibbotson.com/research, December 1998, revised April 1999. "Asset Allocation: Revisiting the Debate." Morningstar, February 27, 1997.

Jahnke, William. "The Asset Allocation Hoax." *Journal of Financial Planning*, February 1997.

Krass, Stephen J. *Pension Answer Book*. Fredrick, MD: Aspen Publishers, 2011.

Morningstar Principia Mutual Funds. March 2006.

Perdue, Grady, PhD, CFP, and Joseph P. McCormack, PhD, CFA. "Don't Drop the Ball on Deferred Retirement Option Plans." *Journal of Financial Planning*, February 2000.

Risk Profile Questionnaire. H.D. Vest Investment Services Inc. 2004.

Singer, Brian. "Hoax and Strawmen." *Journal of Financial Planning*, October 1997.

Statman, Meir. "The Numbers Racket Rages On." *Financial Planning*, April 1998.

US Department of Health, Education and Welfare. "Vital Statistics of the United States, 1970 Volume II–Section 5 Life Tables," Public Health Service, Health Resources Administration, National Center for Health Statistics.

Wilson, Philip. "Mad as Hell." *Dow Jones Investment Advisor*, February 1998.

INDEX